Pastoral Care
of Battered Women

Pastoral Care
of Battered Women

Rita-Lou Clarke

The Westminster Press
Philadelphia

Book design by Gene Harris

First edition

Published by The Westminster Press®
Philadelphia, Pennsylvania

PRINTED IN THE UNITED STATES OF AMERICA

9 8 7 6 5 4 3 2 1

Library of Congress Cataloging-in-Publication Data

Clarke, Rita-Lou.
    Pastoral care of battered women.

    Bibliography: p.
    1. Church work with abused women. I. Title.
BV4445.5.C57 1986   261.8′35872   86-5604
ISBN 0-664-24015-1 (pbk.)

Contents

Foreword

This is an important book for you if you are in one or more of the following categories: pastors and lay leaders of congregations, seminarians and seminary teachers, persons concerned about preventing and healing violence against women and children in their churches and communities, those concerned with the complex interdependencies between personal and societal problems (and between the personal and prophetic dimensions of ministry), advocates of the full liberation of both women and men from the crippling impact of our culture's pervasive sexism, and persons committed to helping pastoral care become more relevant to the forgotten victims of a patriarchal society's widespread violence.

The focus of this book—battered women—is a huge part of the overall problem of domestic violence, a tragedy that has reached epidemic proportions in our society. Traumatic, shattering acts of violence—including spouse beating and homicide, child battering and sexual molestation, sexual harassment and rape—occur with staggeringly high frequency in all socio-economic-educational classes and in all religious groups. (Yes, even in "respectable" neighborhoods and congregations and families, including clergy families!) Yet in spite of their pervasiveness and the deep pain and destructiveness they cause, these issues have received scant attention in the pastoral care literature. This neglect has been owing, in part, to the fact that these gigantic problems have been largely hidden until recent years, when they gradually have been brought out of the closet into the light of public awareness, thanks mainly to the women's movement.

With this book, Rita-Lou Clarke helps in significant ways to fill the yawning gap in the resources of the pastoral care field. In three insightful chapters she provides a lucid understanding of the interrelated cultural, psychological, and theological causes of violence against women. Such violence—physical, psychological, sexual, and spiritual—is the logical and psychological consequence of our culture's sexist ways of socializing boys and girls. Clarke provides abundant evidence demonstrating that traditional sex-role definitions and understandings of the family in patriarchal cultures such as ours set the stage for wife battering. On the one hand, the "learned helplessness" and passivity in relating to males which females are taught by our society make them easy targets of male violence. On the other hand, training males to feel strong and successful only when they are on top of the heap in the success hierarchy, and are dominating those who are socially defined as less powerful, makes women and children the logical target of the aggression and rage stemming from widespread male feelings of failure and impotence. The cycle of violence that characterizes the interaction of battering couples is generated from the mutually destructive interaction of females and males who are socially programmed in these ways. From a cultural perspective, violence against women is the result of the injustice and unequal distribution of social status and of economic, political, and legal power between women and men. So far as the prophetic ministry of the church is concerned, the long-range solution to violence against women is the full liberation of women from their one-down status and their alienation from their real strengths, and the full liberation of men from the destructive self-image that defines success as dominance and equates masculinity with male aggression—in hunting, sports, and the competitive marketplace, in war, and in relations with women and children.

Furthermore, the author demonstrates in convincing fashion how male-oriented theologies, religious beliefs, and church practices derived from sexist interpretation of certain biblical passages tend to foster violence against women. These beliefs, when internalized by women, reinforce their sense of powerlessness and encourage them to stay trapped in battering relationships. The need to liberate theology, religious beliefs, and biblical understanding from male-serving male interpretations becomes clear in the discussion of the way these have been used to keep women "in their place"—including the place of psychological and physical violence against their personhood!

Traditional psychotherapy and most marriage counseling are seen by the author as generally detrimental to battered women and unsuccessful in interrupting the battering cycle. Most attempts to change batterers through individual counseling and psychotherapy also have proved to be ineffective. The importance of consciousness-raising, support groups, and shelters for battered women is emphasized, as is the use of counseling approaches from feminist therapy and from new modes of conjoint counseling for couples trapped in cycles of violent interaction. The need for clergy, especially male clergy, to have our consciousness raised about battering and about the destructiveness of traditional attitudes toward women is highlighted by the author.

The concluding "how to" chapter offers a variety of valuable approaches to pastoral care and counseling with battered women. Practical guidelines are given for educating a congregation regarding the domestic violence problem, handling battering crises, counseling battered women and battering couples, and reaching out in the community to support shelters for women and children who are victims of domestic violence. Particularly helpful is the way in which these guidelines are illuminated by verbatim examples of constructive pastoral care and counseling in such situations. A list of resources and organizations which are useful in developing consciousness-raising and helping arrange programs on domestic violence in congregations is included at the end of the book.

Rita-Lou Clarke, Associate Pastor of the First Presbyterian Church of Garden Grove, California, writes with a pastoral orientation and sensitivity to the painful issues she discusses. Her understanding of the problem of battered women emerges from her experiences as a woman growing up in a sexist society. Her rigorous researching of the problem of battering (a process I had opportunity to observe and value) is clearly reflected in the book's many helpful insights grounded in sound theological and psychosocial understanding. As one of her mentors, I have a warm appreciation of her deep and disciplined concern for battered families and am very pleased that the findings of her study are now available to a wider readership.

As I reflected on the causes and dynamics of violence against women and children as spelled out in the pages that follow, a disturbing awareness gradually came into focus for me. It became clear that to examine this problem in depth is to look through a window into the wider issues and suffering caused in our culture by its pervasive sexism and hierarchical male power arrangements, and its patriarchal religious beliefs, practices, and institutions. This book will enable you to look through that window.

The emerging truth about the prevalence of violence in intimate relationships in our society is a grim and staggering picture. There is no doubt that only the surface has been scratched in either the full treatment or the effective prevention of this societal malignancy. Though the size of the challenge is staggering, there also seem to be some small rays of hope in this darkness. The fact that the problem is being faced more fully than ever before in human history (though still not nearly fully enough) is one such ray. Another is the gradually increasing numbers of people in churches and communities who are beginning to face the challenge and the need to make basic changes in our churches and society in order to reduce and heal the violence. As you read these pages, I trust that you will share the gratitude I feel that this book confronts us with the challenge and describes some promising paths along which pastors and congregations can walk out of the darkness. In short, this book is one of the rays of light and hope!

HOWARD CLINEBELL

Acknowledgments

I am indebted to many for the successful completion of this book.

Thanks go first of all to my husband, Jim, who encouraged and supported me in finishing the doctoral project out of which this book came. He worked on the computer, editing, checking spelling, and printing countless revisions. He listened to me as I expressed my thoughts and ideas; they came to life in the hours of dialogue we had and in his belief that I could make a contribution by writing.

Thanks go to my four children, who heard my ideas and research as I studied in the field and lived in the world of battered women. Thanks go especially to my daughter Janis, who was with us during the summer of the doctoral project and who edited and supported me with "Come on, Mama, you can do it!"

Thanks go to my professors at the School of Theology at Claremont, especially Dr. Howard Clinebell, professor of pastoral counseling, which was my area of concentration. Howard encouraged me throughout my seminary career and chaired my doctoral project committee. He especially supported my work in the field of domestic violence and encouraged me to submit the Doctor of Ministry project for publication. Thanks go to Dr. Jane Dempsey Douglass, professor of church history. Jane was the other faculty member on my committee, and she made sure of the quality of the doctoral project. She checked my logic and documentation, so that there were very few changes needed for publication. And thanks go also to Dr. Dan Rhoades, professor of ethics, who encouraged me to choose the subject of battered women for my Doctor of Ministry project.

Introduction

The battered woman lives in fear. She never knows when
her husband will punch her in the face for wearing the
"wrong" makeup, slap her for fixing a casserole instead of
chicken for dinner, beat her for having a different view
about politics, or threaten her because he had a bad day.
She has tried to get help from pastor, doctor, police, and
friends, but all of them have found a way to blame her and
vindicate her husband. She has no place to go with her
three small children.

The number of battered women in the United States
is unknown. Several researchers have tried to discover
how many women are living in battering relationships.
Their discoveries indicate a very large number. A survey
by sociologists Murray Straus, Richard Gelles, and Suzanne
Steinmetz[1] indicated that almost 2 million, or about 1 of
every 26 (3.8%), American wives get beaten by their husbands every year. If you consider the entire lifetime of the
marriage, one of four husbands are violent to their wives at
some time.

Researchers believe this figure is low. First, there are
some people who underrate violence in the family; they
may not consider a slap to be violence. Second, there are
some who fail to report extreme acts of violence because of
shame or guilt. Third, divorced couples, where there often
is excessive violence, were not sampled. Because of these
factors, researchers place the true rate at closer to 50 to 60
percent. Lenore Walker writes of a New York attorney who

reported that of 500 women she represented in divorce actions in Brooklyn in 1976, 57.4 percent complained of physical assaults by their husbands.[2]

Diana Russell, in *Rape in Marriage,* reports a 21-percent rate of wife beating in her survey. She also reports the results of a study done by Irene Frieze in 1980. Using self-reported battered women and a matching control group, Frieze discovered that 34 percent of the women had experienced violence from their husbands in their marriages.[3] While these samplings of surveys show different results, the studies do reveal a large number of battered women, indicating a serious social problem.

Although wife beating has been with us for centuries, it has been kept behind closed doors in the sanctity of the family. The recognition of wife abuse as a family and social problem came as a consequence of the women's movement and the establishment of shelters for battered women in the late 1960s and 1970s. By 1980, laws were being rewritten and research in prevention and treatment programs was being initiated.

Lenore Walker, in her important book *The Battered Woman,* explodes some of the myths we have had about wife beating. Battering is not a phenomenon only of the poor, the criminal, or the psychotic. Battering is found in all socioeconomic classes and all religious groups, in families that would appear "normal."[4] Battered women are in our churches hidden behind dark glasses and long sleeves with wounded egos and damaged self-esteem.

As more and more women risk getting help for their abusive situations, many will turn to their pastors for help. These pastors need to be able to understand the situations of the women and the factors that brought them there. They need to understand the nature of the violent relationship and what keeps the victim in it. These pastors need to develop knowledge and skills to help women build their damaged self-esteem and overcome the effects of the violence done to them.

The battered woman may be part of a family composed

of spouse and children. Family therapy and marriage counseling have shown us that the family and the married couple are systems that work as units. Pastors and counselors need to understand more about the patterns and dynamics of violence in the family and marriage so we can find effective ways of confronting it and of bringing the couple and family to a new way of relating that is mutually supportive, redemptive, and whole.

Certain cultural and religious images of marriage, sex roles, and family life encourage women to stay in the battering situation. Pastors and counselors need to be aware of these images so that they do not continue to reinforce them in counseling. They need to put forth new images of personhood and marriage that are redemptive and liberating. The marriage needs to be transformed from one of abuse and violence to one of peace, justice, and mercy.

Focus of the Problem

The behavior I am focusing on in this book is the act of a husband battering his wife—striking her hard and repeatedly, with bruising, shattering blows. It is important to determine who is responsible for the specific act of violence. Although the woman may contribute to the poor communication in the marriage, or may remain in the relationship after her husband has beaten her, therefore implicitly giving permission for him to hit her again, she does not cause him to hit her. The woman may appear to provoke, she may be unpleasant and act badly, she may be a "bitch," but she is still not responsible for his act of violence. No one deserves to be beaten.

In some states it is against the law for a teacher to hit a student. No matter how rebellious, obnoxious, obstreperous, or unmanageable the child may be, the law declares that the teacher may not hit the child. The teacher is responsible for finding ways to deal with the child that are not violent. The court in this case will not consider any excuses of the teacher about the extenuating circumstances that may have "made" him or her hit the child. The fact is, the teacher may not hit the child under *any* circumstances.

We as a society have not yet come to the place where we declare unequivocally that a man may not hit his wife under any circumstances. The recent changes in the law making wife battery illegal indicate a movement in that direction. We still need changes in attitude that will make it possible for police, attorneys, judges, social workers, pastors, and counselors to play their part in stopping the approval of wife beating. In no circumstance is a man justified in hitting his wife. That does not mean that the wife should not make changes in her behavior. It only means that she is not responsible for his act of hitting. For the marriage to be repaired, the hitting must stop. Then both the husband and the wife can work together to build a better marriage.

Psychological battering is related to and accompanies physical battering but is much more elusive because there is no direct physical impact. Application of the dynamics of physical battering may be applied to psychological battering. There is still no excuse for the psychological attack.

In viewing the woman as victim in the battering incident, we are changing from the longtime view of woman as instigator of the violence against her. We still have the old view with us in thoughts and statements as "What did you do to provoke him?" "She deserved it!" "Why does she stay? She must get something out of it." I am not saying that the woman is innocent or should be self-righteous in the situation. I am emphasizing woman as victim to effect a change in our perception about the beaten woman's role.

Limitation of This Book

The subject of domestic violence covers such issues as spouse abuse, battered women, child abuse, incest, marital rape, and parent abuse. I am choosing to focus specifically on pastoral care of battered women for three reasons. First, it is usually the woman victim who seeks help from her pastor or counselor. Second, many times the male batterer is resistant to joining his wife or partner in seeking help, so that the pastor or counselor is limited to working with the woman. Third, if the woman is helped in her battering situation, the children, who may be experiencing abuse by the woman or her batterer—or both—will be helped.

Although husbands can be the recipients of violence by wives, I have chosen to focus on wives as victims of violence by their husbands for several reasons, which are documented by studies done in the field.

1. Much of a wife's violence toward her husband is a response to *his* violence toward her. She is protecting herself or retaliating in violence after sometimes years of violence done to her.

2. Abuse by husbands does more physical damage than a wife's violence toward her husband. The man's greater strength makes it likely that a woman will be more seriously injured when beaten by her husband.

3. Husbands have higher rates of using the most dangerous weapons, such as knives and guns.

4. When violent acts are committed by a husband, they are repeated more often than is the case for wives.

5. A large number of violent attacks by husbands occur when the wife is pregnant, endangering the unborn child as well.

6. In a traditional marriage the wife is more bound economically and socially. If she has children she is doubly bound, since in this kind of marriage, the wife is almost always the primary caregiver of children.[5]

Traditional ideology and patriarchal values support the existence of wife beating. The church has tended to allow patriarchal myths and values to influence its theology. As pastors and counselors, we need to challenge our theology to make it liberating for all, rather than oppressive to some. We need to develop practical ways to help women who are caught in battering situations. So the church needs to accept its responsibility to recognize and intervene in the growing awareness of wife abuse.

Definition of Major Terms

Many of the terms involved become ambiguous when used by the press and the media. The following definitions will clarify what is meant by the terms used here.

Battered Woman: A battered woman is a woman who is repeatedly subjected to any forceful physical or psychological behavior by a man in order to coerce her to do something he wants her to do without any concern for her rights. Battered women may be wives or other women in intimate relationships with men. Furthermore, in order for a woman to be classified as battered, the couple must go through the battering cycle at least twice.[6]

Feminism: Feminism is an ideological commitment to the legal, economic, and social equality of the sexes. It does not seek to replace male supremacy with female supremacy or patriarchy with matriarchy. Rather, a feminist is any person, female or male, who envisions and works toward equal rights, opportunity, and human dignity for all.[7]

Patriarchy: Patriarchy is a social organization headed by the father and recognizing the male line of descent. In the larger political sense—that is, wherever power relationships are involved—patriarchy is any system that runs on a hierarchical principle, with the "top man" invested with absolute power over those under him.[8]

Sexism: Sexism is bias, prejudice, or discrimination based on gender. A sexist has preconceptions about female human beings—usually negative generalizations regarding their inferiority to male human beings. Because sexism is a deeply entrenched, often unconscious cultural attitude, many of us are unaware that we may be classifying someone's temperament, capabilities, or interests according to stereotyped expectations of what women and men or girls and boys are like.[9]

1
The Battered Woman in the Cultural Context

Wife battering did not become widely recognized as a social problem in American life until the late 1970s. This recognition came as a result of the women's movement. In the late 1960s, when women began to meet together in groups to discuss women's issues and to support each other, they discovered a common problem of violence in their families. These women had thought they were the only ones who were being beaten and believed that they "deserved it" or "asked for it." In groups, they found that many other women had similar experiences and feelings.

In the mid-seventies, the National Organization for Women (NOW) decided to make battered wives a priority issue. Women's groups across the United States began a political effort to establish better social services for battered wives and to force changes in laws that denied women adequate legal redress from being beaten by their husbands. In 1976, Del Martin published her important book *Battered Wives,* an early major study of wife abuse.[1]

Neighborhood centers for women grew out of the women's movement in England. One such center led to the first shelter or "safe house" for abused wives. Its founder, Erin Pizzey, later described this first battered-wife refuge in *Scream Quietly or the Neighbors Will Hear,* written in 1974.[2]

The beginnings of shelters for abused women in the United States came from a grass-roots movement initiated and supported by women. These shelters began and now

exist on limited funds and shoestring budgets. Many of
them are operated by women who were abused themselves
and were successful in extricating themselves from battering relationships. These women are able in turn to help
other women overcome their battering situations. The shelters also make provisions for the children of women who
come to them for help.

Women who are abused by their husbands are found in
all socioeconomic classes, at all educational levels, and in
all religious groups.[3] We have the impression that wife
battering is greater among persons of the lower socioeconomic classes because these women are the ones who go to
shelters and get involved with the police, where there would
be a record of their abuse. The poor have fewer resources
than the middle and upper classes, but no group is immune
from the problem.

We are in a period of great change in our society. The
civil rights movement of the 1960s, the recognition of child
abuse, the peace movement, the women's movement, and
the recognition of the extent of domestic violence have all
been factors in helping us recognize the rights of all persons
regardless of race, sex, age, or nationality. Affirming the
rights of particular groups challenges some of our cultural
myths and beliefs.

We have discovered that the phenomenon of wife beating
has existed throughout history and continues to be resistant
to change because some very strong cultural myths and
images support it. To change the practice of wife beating
we must change the basic myths. We will begin by naming
them and calling them into question: patriarchy, sexism,
and violence as a way of life.

Patriarchy

When we look at the extent and pervasiveness of wife
abuse, we must conclude that it is not just a problem of
marital misadjustment or personality maladjustment of a
few. Social scientists and psychologists working in the field

of battered women are in agreement in their view of patriarchy and its effect on wife abuse. As Mildred Pagelow states, "These writers have generally singled out as the starting point for a theory of wife abuse the patriarchal foundations of the family itself and the hierarchical power structure that provides the framework of modern social systems."[4]

Terry Davidson gives an excellent short account of wife beating as it recurs throughout patriarchal history. In pre-patriarchal history women were revered for their ability to give birth. Davidson evaluates the beginnings of patriarchy. "Once man realized the significance of his participation in coitus, however, man's religious status gradually changed as a woman's status gradually became debased. As man became the Patriarch, society did an about-face toward a repressive mode of living."[5]

Emerson and Russell Dobash, in studies completed in 1979, conclude that the hierarchical structure of the patriarchal family has legitimized wife beating to subordinate, dominate, and control women. The institutions of church and state supported the patriarchal tradition and resisted any change in the status of women suggested by such reformers as Abigail Adams, John Stuart Mill, and Elizabeth Cady Stanton. The cultural belief was that men had the right to dominate and control women and that women were by their nature subservient to men.[6]

A part of Pagelow's hypothesis in her study of battered women was that the more intensely a woman believed traditional ideology, the more likely she was to remain in relationship with her batterer and the less likely she would be to act in such a way as to significantly alter her situation in a positive way. Pagelow defines traditional ideology:

> Traditional ideology encompasses a broad range of internalized beliefs favoring acceptance of the rightness of the patriarchal-hierarchal order of the social structure. It is a set of beliefs and attitudes that is a fundamental part of the way persons evaluate life and circumstances and serves to guide and motivate behavior. Traditional ideology is the configura-

tion of all the conservative wisdom passed down through the ages as the inherent "natural" order of things.[7]

Pagelow wondered why it was that shelters were having such a hard time being established and funded and why there was such resistance to helping a battered woman. She concluded that the availability of a safe place where a woman could find an escape from her violent marriage was seen as a threat to two of our basic institutions, marriage and the family (p. 217). Terry Davidson quoted an attorney who was with a shelter group:

> We weren't prepared to handle the unexpected red herring. The opposition was economic, political, and religious, claiming, "If we give money to feminists, they will encourage women to leave their homes and destroy the Christian family." What is sorely needed now is people who are in religion saying, "But the church doesn't support wife-beating. It's the batterer that destroys the family."[8]

Lenore Walker believes that we are in a changing time, during which patriarchy will be replaced by egalitarianism, equality among people. She continues, "Probably the reason the women's movement has elicited such great fear is that it is correctly perceived as the beginning of this revolution. A cornerstone, then, of the creation of a new egalitarian social order would be to reverse the tides of violence committed against women" (p. 12).

Patriarchy provides a social structure of ownership of women by men which makes it possible for men to do whatever they want with their women. Del Martin, in *Battered Wives,* carefully researched the history of patriarchy to show how that system has allowed and encouraged husbands to beat, stab, shoot, choke, rape, and kill their wives (chapter 3). A film was recently produced about men who batter. Several men were given an opportunity to tell their stories. A consistent theme emerged: Each man had a prevailing belief that he "owned" his wife.[9]

If a man legally owns a woman in marriage to protect his paternity, he has the right to control her forcefully even to the extent of physical violence. John Stuart Mill, a nineteenth-century philosopher, wrote:

> From the very earliest twilight of human society, every woman
> . . . was found in a state of bondage to some man. . . . Men
> are not required as a preliminary in marriage to prove that
> they are fit to be trusted with absolute power over another
> human being. . . . The vilest malefactor has some wretched
> woman tied to him, against whom he can commit any atroc-
> ity except killing her—and even that he can do without too
> much danger of legal penalty.[10]

English common-law doctrine allowed the husband "the right to whip his wife, provided that he used a switch no bigger than his thumb." This was known as the "rule of thumb" law.[11]

The trend in the early United States was to make wife beating illegal, and this direction has continued. An 1824 Mississippi decision allowed the husband to administer only "moderate chastisement in cases of emergency." By 1894 even that right was ruled illegal in Mississippi.[12] By 1975 most states in our country had laws permitting a wife to bring criminal action against a husband who injured her physically. Before the enactment of these laws, if a man struck a stranger on the street he would be arrested for assault and battery. But if he beat his wife in private *or* on the street, the law and society condoned it. Remember the incident in the streets of Queens, New York, in 1964 when Kitty Genovese was beaten to death by an attacker. Neighbors saw the incident but pulled their shades because they thought the pair were husband and wife having a marital fight.[13]

Law enforcement has not kept up with legal changes. Believing that "a man's home is his castle," many police refuse to interfere in domestic violence cases. When one woman called 911 to complain that her husband had beaten her and then pushed her down the stairs, the policeman said, "Listen, lady, he pays the bills, doesn't he? What he does inside his own house is his business."[14] This belief also enables judges to refuse to rule on wife-battering cases, telling the couple only to "go home and settle your differences."

Ann Jones, author of *Women Who Kill,* observes that with every push for women's rights comes a wave of attention to women's criminality. The implicit assumption is that free women are dangerous women because they are stepping out of the "role" set for them as "women." Jones's observation is that dangerous women are ordinary women who are trying to find a way out of a bad situation. She writes, "Women who kill find extreme solutions to problems that thousands of women cope with in more peaceable ways from day to day."[15]

When attention began to be paid to the plight of battered women, a backlash of concern arose about the plight of battered men, which reached its apex in the media in February of 1978. There was a push for shelters for battered men, but none were established, and for a time the women's shelter movement suffered. As Jones evaluates the results of the battered-husband bandwagon, "Most important, the battered-husband hype which equated husband-beating with wife-beating obscured and trivialized the massive problem of wife abuse" (p. 302). Three reputable sociologists in the field of domestic violence, Suzanne Steinmetz, Richard Gelles, and Murray Straus, were drawn into the battered-husband issue for a period of time. They soon corrected themselves, and in a later publication they gave six reasons why wife abuse is more critical than husband abuse.[16]

The model of authority for patriarchy is hierarchical. In this pattern, authority comes from the top down. The man is the head of the family, and the wife is the obedient support person. A recent study showed that "wife beating is much more common in homes where power is concentrated in the hands of the husband." The rate for wife beating went from less than 2 percent in democratic households to more than 20 percent in husband-dominated households.[17] In democratic households there was less battering. If our culture approves of the hierarchical model, which puts power in the hands of the husband, that power also gives him sanction to punish those who resist his attempts to control them (the wife and children). The inequality in a hierarchical family may initiate a chain reaction running throughout the family. If the husband hits his wife, she may not strike back for fear of suffering greater violence. She may instead hit the children, who in turn lash out at weaker brothers and sisters, who may then abuse the cat or dog.

Sexism

Sexism is a word that came into being in 1970. The word follows the dictionary definition of "racism." As racism is a belief that race is a primary determinant of human traits, so sexism is a belief that sex is a primary determinant of human traits and capacities and that sexual differences produce an inherent superiority of one sex. Sexism is discrimination based on sexual prejudice, particularly against women.

The traditional ideology of the patriarchal structure views husband and wife as having particular and separate functions. The husband protects and provides for the family. In our culture he should go outside the home to work. He should be the one who makes the decisions, especially the important ones, as ruler/owner of the wife and children. The wife bears and nurtures the children. She should make a nest for the family and be subject to her lord-and-master husband. These patriarchal role expectations for husband and wife have become clearly defined.

When the battered woman and her husband accept these role expectations, an environment favoring battering has been created. If the husband believes he is to be the provider but cannot get a job and support his family, he may believe he is inadequate. Even if the wife has a better-paying job and can support the family, the husband still feels it is his duty to be "breadwinner." The lowered self-esteem and stress from feeling inadequate may make the husband more prone to violence. He believes the wife must fulfill her domestic duties or she is not an adequate wife. If she does not fulfill them to the husband's expectation, he may beat her.

A 1979 study supported earlier findings of Straus and others. Violence by the husband and not by the wife was found to be dependent on three factors:

1. The husband being dominant in family decisions
2. The wife being a full-time housewife
3. The wife being very worried about economic security[18]

The sexist economic and occupational structure of society puts the woman in this kind of family at a severe disadvantage. The battered wife tends to be a full-time homemaker. She has not been trained for a career because she was planning to be married. She offers little resistance to her husband's violence because she is economically dependent upon him. If she were to look for a job, the ones that are open to her are lower in status and pay less than for a man with similar education.

Violence as a Way of Life

The work of Straus, Gelles, and Steinmetz in 1976, as reported in *Behind Closed Doors,* represents the first comprehensive national study of violence in the American family. There were 2143 families interviewed, representative of the approximately 46 million families in the United States. The goals were to uncover the breadth of family violence, to measure its extent, to find out what the violence meant to the participants, and to assess why it took place.

The authors concluded that a person runs a greater risk of assault, physical injury, and even murder in one's own home than in any other setting. They estimated that police answer more calls involving family conflicts than all other criminal incidents combined, including murders, rapes, robberies, nonfamily assaults, and muggings.

The researchers also reported on the American public's degree of approval of violence, noting that the U.S. National Commission on the Causes and Prevention of Violence found in 1970 that one out of four men and one out of six women surveyed approved of a husband's slapping a wife under certain conditions. Another sociologist, Maria Roy, reported that, according to a Harris Poll, 20 percent of all Americans approve of hitting a spouse on appropriate occasions. Among college-educated people, the rate was 25 percent.[19]

Although many people do not consider spanking a child to be a form of violence, Straus, Gelles, and Steinmetz included it. Some parents argue that spanking is for the child's own good. They support their argument with quotes from scripture along the theme of "spare the rod and spoil the child" (Prov. 13:24; 19:18; 22:15; 23:13–14; 29:15–17). There is a long religious tradition in America, beginning with the arrival of the Puritans, for parents to use physical punishment on children to enable them to gain salvation. To "beat the devil" out of a child was a serious mandate.[20]

Studies in both the United States and England revealed that 84 percent to 97 percent of all parents still use physical punishment at some time in their child's life. These studies also showed that the persons most likely to be struck are typically the smallest, weakest members. Over 70 percent of Americans believe that spanking a twelve-year-old child is necessary, normal, or good. In the interviews the researchers conducted, parents indicated that they slap or spank a child hard enough to get the child to stop doing what the parent does not want done.

INTERVIEWER: When do you slap or spank your child?

PARENT: When I want her to stop something . . . like when I want her to get away from the stove.

INTERVIEWER: How hard do you hit her?

PARENT: Hard enough to get her to stop.

INTERVIEWER: You mean if the first slap doesn't get her to stop—

PARENT: I hit her again, a little harder.[21]

Since most of us have experienced violence as children in that most intimate of relationships, the family, the researchers concluded that we learn certain lessons from the experience.

    1. Those who love you the most are also those who hit you. It is normal and acceptable.

    2. Using physical punishment on children to secure a "good" end—i.e., training in morally correct behavior or teaching the child to avoid injury—teaches the moral rightness of violence.

    3. Violence is permissible when other things don't work.

There is strong evidence that children who observe their parents being violent to each other tend to be violent when they themselves marry. Parents who were subjected to a great deal of physical punishment as children have the highest rates of abusive violence toward their own children and each other. The whole atmosphere of approval and practice of violence in the home toward children, and to others who are smaller and weaker, sets an environment for wife beating to occur and persist.[22]

Other Factors That Affect the Extent of Violence

Stress increases the incidence of violence. The study showed that wife abuse increased proportionately with the number of children living at home, up to six. Spouse abuse was less for couples with no children. The families in the survey were polled for the number of major stresses they had experienced. There was a high correlation between the amount of stress and the level of spouse abuse.[23]

Women are highly vulnerable to being physically abused during pregnancy. A study by Richard Gelles in 1975 showed that one fourth of the women who were battered by their husbands were struck during pregnancy. As one woman said, "Oh, yeah, he hit me when I was pregnant. It was weird. Usually he just hit me in the face with his fist, but when I was pregnant he used to hit me in the belly. It was weird."[24]

The stress of the outside world and problems encountered there by the husband may be translated into violence against the wife when he arrives home. Why would a man beat his wife when he is unemployed or has had a bad day at work? It is more socially acceptable for him to beat his wife than to hit someone at work. Besides, he can get away with beating his wife. He can't get away with hitting his boss. When a man feels threatened and devalued at work, at least he can feel "like a man" at home. He can exercise his authority and mastery by using force and violence against his wife.

The use of alcohol is a way of life for the majority of Americans. We have ads promoting the "good life" associated with alcohol. Social drinking is acceptable behavior. Along with this is the myth that one is not responsible for what one does under the influence of alcohol. Gelles indicates that there is a strong correlation between alcoholism and violence.[25] Alcoholics tend to beat their wives. Alcohol gives them an excuse to be violent when they would not be at other times. One wife reports: "He hit me many times. But at first, like I say, it was only when he was drinking . . . he wouldn't even slap me when he was sober no matter how mad he got."[26]

Institutional Resources

Mildred Pagelow found a correlation between institutional response to a battered woman and her likelihood of staying in the abusive relationship while doing nothing to help herself. If she received negative response from legal, medical, or religious institutions, she was less likely to act positively to alter her situation.[27]

Almost all institutions traditionally try to reconcile the family. They work to keep the family together "at all costs."

There is a popular assumption that intact families represent stability and that dissolution means failure or breakdown in the family system.[28]

Even though it is against the law in many states for a man to assault his wife, when a battered woman calls the police department, she is typically met with the attitude that the problem is one of domestic squabbling. Police officers try to calm the couple. Commander James Bannon of the Detroit Police Department has evaluated the competency of the police:

> This paradox suggests to me that traditionally trained and socialized policemen are the worst possible choice to attempt to intervene in domestic violence. . . . In my view the police attitude, which seems to say that what happens between man and wife in their own home is beyond the authority or ability of the police to control, is a "cop out." The real reason that police avoid domestic violence situations to the greatest extent possible is because we do not know how to cope with them. And besides we share [society's] views that domestic violence is an individual problem and not a public issue.[29]

Police become very discouraged with the battered woman when she does not press charges. Pagelow discovered some reasons for this failure to follow through from the women in her survey. First of all, women are ignorant of their civil rights and are almost never encouraged to demand them. Second, they are persuaded not to demand equal justice under the law. Police encourage the wife to take the children and leave home rather than get the husband to leave. Third, women have little or no protection against retaliation by their husbands, except for recently established shelters, and then for only thirty days.[30]

Fortunately, some police departments are giving special training for handling domestic violence cases. They are helping women get to shelters. In some cases they are pressing charges against the batterers themselves, which new laws allow them to do.

Middle-class women who are beaten by their husbands are usually able to go to private doctors to be treated.

Pagelow interviewed one medical doctor who practiced in an affluent neighborhood. He described himself as "neutral" (pp. 69–70):

> Many of my middle class patients who come to me with suspicious wounds make up some cock-and-bull story of how they got hurt. But, yes, I've seen women who come in for treatment of injuries they claimed were given to them by their husbands. A lot of them are repeaters; they come back time and again. I ask them why they put up with it, and they can't give any good answers. It may be a matter of money, maybe they figure they'd lose out by leaving. I don't understand it—they just don't make sense. There's nothing you can do for them.

It seems to be common practice in such situations for physicians and psychiatrists to prescribe tranquilizers. This is evidenced by the large number of women who come to the shelters with prescribed drugs. Being tranquilized is the worst possible condition for a battered woman. She needs to be alert to be better able to avert a possible beating and to control her situation.[31]

Many battered women seek advice from their pastors, often to be told that they should "go home and forgive him." Terry Davidson's criticism of the clergy in 1978 was this:

> The clergy preaches a male-oriented theology and structure of the marriage relationship. The clergy has not been in the vanguard of help for the battered wife. Instead, its attitudes about woman's place, duty, and nature have added to the problem. Even now, with few exceptions, the silence from the churches on this issue is profound.[32]

Davidson (p. 211) quotes Ellen Kirby of the Board of Global Ministries of the United Methodist Church as she spoke on the issue:

> The abuse of women . . . should be a major focus of concern for religious institutions in the next decade or until this terrible problem is eradicated from our society. . . . Unfortunately . . . the institutional church either through its blatant sexist theology, which has blessed the subordination of women,

or through its silence, blindness, or lack of courage, has allowed itself to be one of the leading actors in the continuing tragedy of abuse.

Most of the denominations now have literature about wife abuse, and many support shelters for battered women. As pastors become aware and educated, they will be more helpful to the battered women in their churches.

Future Hopes for the Culture

The women's movement has begun to raise our consciousness about the problem of abused wives. Changes have come that bring hope to battered women. We must, as a church, continue to influence the structures of society by changing the beliefs about male/female relationships from hierarchical to egalitarian and from domination to liberation.

We must change the beliefs that make violence acceptable and legitimate in our society. First is the belief that spanking children is necessary, good, and beneficial. Professionals in the fields of child development and education seriously question spanking and other physical violence as options in discipline. Researchers in both these fields are working on new ways to teach and discipline children without resorting to physical violence. Second is the availability of firearms. Free access to guns makes these weapons handy to be used against wives. Third is the glorification of violence on television. This persistent model of violence as a way to solve problems continues to support violence as a way of life.

We must change the sexist and patriarchal character of society and the family. "As long as we expect men to head the family because they are men, and women to care for children because they are women, we are going to have potential conflict and violence in homes."[33] We need to make the family an egalitarian institution where jobs and tasks are chosen on the basis of ability and interest rather than on sex. Decision-making and household tasks need to be shared.

We must support shelter programs, which offer refuge to a victim when she has no other place to go. Being in a shelter with others who have had similar experiences helps a woman know that she is not alone and that she has support. It helps her to be aware of the options she has in life and to regain some of the self-esteem she has lost from being in an abusive situation. Even if a woman chooses to go back into a battering relationship, she goes back a little stronger for having had the shelter experience.

The battered woman has been influenced by her culture to accept violence toward her by her husband as normal. But such long-standing forces are now being challenged in favor of a new valuing of the role and position of wife. We who are in a position to pastor and counsel the battered woman have an opportunity to offer sanctuary during change, healing of the wounds, and new beginnings of life.

2
The Psychological Dimension of Battering

In dealing with the psychological dimension of battering, I will be focusing on the dynamics of the battering couple. I will be drawing largely upon the work of Lenore Walker, a psychologist with a feminist point of view, who began to study battered women in 1975. Walker was one of the first psychologists to study the psychology of battered women as victims. She reported the results of her work in *The Battered Woman,* published in 1979.

The traditional theory about battering had been that women participated in their own victimization—that somehow they "asked for it." The battered woman was thought to be masochistic and her man to be sadistic and violent in all his behavior. Traditional theorists regarded such aggressiveness as natural. The women's movement had pointed out the huge amount of violence being committed against women by men. Walker's feminist analysis was that sexism and the power differential between men and women is at the bottom of all violence against women.[1]

In her search to explore the woman as victim in the battering relationship, Walker set out to interview women of all ages and walks of life. She chose to listen to the women themselves to see what she could learn. She collected over 120 detailed stories and listened to fragments of 300 more.

Walker found her ability to listen without blaming the victim a great asset. The women had rarely been able to find a listener who would hear them out. As Walker declares:

Most listeners would cut them off as soon as they got to some of the more ghastly details. Either they were *not believed* or they were told that it could only be assumed that they liked what was happening to them, since they had not left the violent situation that they were in. But the *pain* these women experienced in retelling their stories was testimony enough that *none of them had a deep psychological need to be battered.*[2]

The women Walker saw came from shelters and safe houses in the United States and England. They volunteered to be interviewed. Because the sample was not random, Walker could not use statistics of the interviews to support generalizations about battered women. Instead, she concentrated on the commonalities expressed by the battered women and generalized from them. From the listening came understanding.

A woman was considered to be battered if she declared herself to be. She was considered battered if she had been abused more than once in a relationship with a man. If she had been beaten once and stayed and was beaten a second time, she was considered battered. She must have gone through the battering cycle at least twice.

Learned Helplessness

Walker found that most of the research on family violence tended to focus on the pathology of the man and woman involved and on the intrapsychic conflicts or internal personality problems of each. Psychologists concluded, when they observed women repeatedly going back to battering relationships, that there must be some flaw in their personalities. They labeled such women as masochistic in nature, thereby placing the blame on the victim. The men were declared to be mentally ill or psychopathic, which meant absolving them of responsibility for their behavior.[3]

Walker's research led her to conclude that this approach is inadequate. Women do not remain in the battering relationship because they like being beaten. Some stay because they are economically and socially dependent. Others have no safe place to go. Psychologists tend to counsel the family to stay together at all costs, even at the expense of physical and psychological well-being.

Listening to the stories of the women who participated in her survey, Walker observed a three-stage cycle of violence. She developed a psychological rationale which explains why the battered woman becomes a victim and how the process of victimization is perpetuated. The rationale is based on the social-learning theory of "learned helplessness" developed by Martin Seligman.[4]

According to Walker, Seligman asserts that if an individual is caught in a position where repeated attempts to make changes in the environment fail, the individual will learn to be helpless. This helpless state can continue to exist until some external force changes the environment. This situation can cause great anxiety and depression.

Seligman and his researchers put dogs in cages and administered electric shocks at random intervals. When the dogs learned that no matter what they did they could not control the shock, they became compliant, passive, and submissive. When the researchers changed the procedure and tried to teach the dogs that they could escape by crossing to the other side of the cage, the dogs would not respond. Even when the door was left open, the dogs remained passive, refusing to leave to avoid the shock. It took repeated dragging of the dogs to the exit to teach them how to avoid the shock. The earlier in life that the dogs learned to be helpless, the longer it took them to overcome the effects. Once they were retaught that they could avoid the shock, their helplessness faded.

The learned helplessness theory has three basic components: (1) information about what will happen; (2) thinking (learning, expectation, belief, and perception) about what will happen; and (3) reaction toward what does happen. It is the second point, belief or perception, that determines the actions of a given individual. If a woman believes that she cannot control a situation and that she is helpless, she will respond passively and submissively. This perception can become reality. Once a woman believes she cannot control what happens to her, it is difficult for her to believe she can ever influence it, even when she sometimes experiences a favorable outcome.[5]

Walker found that battered women seemed to be most afflicted with feelings of helplessness in their relationships with men. She observed that many women were successful and competent in their careers and other areas of life. It was only when they were relating to the batterer that they exhibited helpless behavior.

In applying the concept of learned helplessness to battered women, we see the process of how the battered woman becomes victimized. Repeated batterings act like electric shocks to diminish the woman's motivation to respond. She becomes passive. Her perception is changed. She believes that nothing she can do will help. She generalizes her helplessness in her relationship so that she is saying to herself, "No matter what I do, I have no influence." Ultimately, her sense of emotional well-being is affected, and she is more prone to anxiety and depression.

Walker contends "the very fact of being a woman, more specifically a married woman, automatically creates a situation of powerlessness."[6] She sees this as one of the detrimental effects of sex-role stereotyping. Women are taught by parents and society that their personal worth is based on their physical beauty and appeal to men rather than their creative responses to life situations. Girls learn to be more passive than boys. Women, then, begin marriage at a psychological disadvantage.

Our patriarchal structure of marriage gives men more power than women. In many states it is not against the law for a man to rape his wife. The husband has legal power to decide where the family will live. Economic realities mean that men more often than women hold higher-paying jobs, which gives them the economic power in the marriage. These men often assume more decision-making power as well. Most men are physically stronger and bigger than women. This greater physical strength, the economic realities, the laws, and cultural conditioning all work like electric shocks to condition women to learned helplessness.

As the dogs were dragged to the exit and to safety, so can
a battered woman learn ways to overcome her battering
situation. Some of this help may come from the outside.
The woman can be persuaded to leave the battering relationship. Safe houses are effective places for her to experience alternative choices. As a battered woman realizes the
power and choice she does have, her strength grows and
her helplessness fades.

The Cycle Theory of Violence

In her interviews with battered women, Walker discovered a definite battering cycle that the women experienced.
This cycle is repeated over and over with each woman in
relationship with her batterer. Understanding it can help
us see how women fall into learned helplessness behavior
and why they do not attempt to escape.

Walker's battering cycle has three distinct phases: (1) the
tension-building phase; (2) the explosion or acute battering
incident; (3) and the calm, loving respite. Walker has not
been able to estimate how long a couple will stay in one
phase. It seems to depend on each couple's unique relationship and what their stage of life is. Walker has found that
certain treatment interventions are more successful if they
occur at one phase rather than another.

Phase one is the tension-building phase, when minor
battering incidents occur. These can be verbal tirades,
throwing things, or temper tantrums. The woman, believing that what she does will prevent her batterer's anger
from escalating, works to control the situation. She may
become loving, compliant, nurturing, and anticipating of
his every whim or she may stay out of his way. If she is
successful, the minor incident will end. If he explodes, she
assumes the guilt. By accepting some of the responsibility
for his abusive behavior, she has become his accomplice.

To keep him from hurting her more she must maintain this role. She must not become angry, so she denies the anger she feels from being unjustly abused physically and psychologically. But the anger is there, under cover. She rationalizes that perhaps she did do something to deserve it, or she is lucky he didn't throw the dish at her instead of the wall, or she justifies him and excuses his behavior by saying to herself, "He had a bad day at work" or "He has been drinking, he can't help it."

As the tension builds, it becomes harder and harder for the woman to deny and control her anger. Her passiveness seems to spur the batterer on. She is not able to put controls on his behavior. Society by its attitude allows him to "discipline" his wife. Most batterers are only violent in their homes because society will not allow them to be violent elsewhere. As the woman becomes more passive, he becomes more possessive and aggressive, until the tension between them becomes unbearable.

Phase two is the acute battering incident, which is characterized by lack of predictability and lack of control. Anticipation of what might occur causes great stress for the woman. She may suffer from sleepless nights, loss of appetite, oversleeping, overeating, or fatigue. She may have severe headaches, stomach ailments, high blood pressure, and other physical responses to the tension.

When the acute battering incident happens, it is entirely in the man's control. The woman has ceased to be able to manipulate the environment to his satisfaction. Both parties accept the fact that his rage is out of control. The batterer starts out by wanting to teach his woman a lesson. He stops when he feels she has learned her lesson. She has no control over when he stops. She experiences disbelief that the incident is really happening to her and dissociates herself from the attack. She endures until it is over.

Those of us who are accustomed to being in control of our lives have a hard time believing that the woman can do nothing to stop her batterer. Indeed, once she becomes aware of her state as a battered wife and begins to try to take charge of her life there are some things she can do in phase two, such as leaving the premises when she sees an attack coming. But when the violence of phase two has begun and the batterer's adrenaline is going full force, there is very little the woman can do to stop him. His anger and strength keep him going. Her fear and state of mind immobilize her.

Many of the reactions battered women report are similar to those of disaster victims, who generally suffer emotional collapse twenty-four to forty-eight hours after a catastrophe. Battered women experience similar symptoms of listlessness, depression, and feelings of helplessness. These victims tend to remain isolated for at least twenty-four hours. It is common for battered women to wait several days before seeking medical aid and help from mental health professionals.

If police are called, it is during phase two. The police try to calm down the batterer and his victim and then leave. This seldom has any effect, for the batterer resumes his violence as soon as the police leave. Police may complain of being attacked by the woman when they attempt to intervene during an acute attack of violence. What the police fail to understand is that the woman knows that when the police leave her batterer will escalate the violence. She is trying to show her loyalty to her man so perhaps he will not resume the beating.

Phase three is characterized by extremely loving, kind, and contrite behavior by the batterer. The batterer is trying to make up for his abusive behavior. It is during this period that the victimization of the woman becomes complete.

The tension that built up in phase one has been released in phase two, so there is a period of calm. The batterer is charming and loving. He begs forgiveness and promises never to do it again. He believes he will never do it again. He believes he can control himself. He believes he has taught her a lesson so she will never behave in such a way as to make him do it again. He promises to reform. He manages to convince everyone involved that he really can do it. This time he means it.

It was at the beginning of phase three that Walker made contact with her battered women. They were most likely to leave the men at the end of the acute battering incident. Many whom she interviewed were in the hospital recovering from injuries inflicted by their batterers. Walker reported on their state of mind:

> Within a few days, they went from being lonely, angry, frightened, and hurt to being happy, confident, and loving. Initially, they had realistically assessed their situations. They accepted their inability to control the batterers' behavior. They were experiencing anger and terror, which helped motivate them to consider making major changes in their lives. These women were thoroughly convinced of their desire to stop being victims, until the batterer arrived. I always knew when a woman's husband had made contact with her by the profusion of flowers, candy, cards, and other gifts in her hospital room.[7]

The batterer uses any means possible to keep his woman: the influence of his family and friends as well as his confessions and promises. All of these play on her guilt. He would fall apart without her. She worries that if she leaves with the children they will be deprived of their father.

The woman is held responsible for any consequences of his behavior by herself, her batterer, and her family and friends. She holds to the traditional values of the permanency of marriage. By such values she thinks, If we love each other, we can conquer all, even this. The batterer needs her. He needs help. The implication is that if she stays with him, he will get that help. Walker has found, however, that the most common time for a batterer to get help is after the woman has left.

The battered woman chooses to believe that the loving behavior she sees during phase three is what he is really like. She chooses to discount the behavior of phase two, the violent attack. Phase three is the time when most helpers see her. Since this is the time when she is experiencing the rewards of the marriage, this is the time when she resists ending the relationship. She really loves him. She hopes, once again, that phases one and two will not happen again. She idealizes the relationship. She sells her psychological and physical safety for a dream. She has become an accomplice to her own battering.

Are all women as helpless as the learned helplessness factor would lead us to believe? Connie Dorn thinks not.[8] The women she observed in 17 out of 21 couples she counseled are knowledgeable of their legal rights, have competent jobs, and do not appear to be victims. The men in these relationships appear to be dependent, impulsive, and intensely possessive of their wives. The wives see themselves as psychologically stronger and more stable than their husbands. These women need to be needed. They fear abandonment more than violence. They see themselves as responsible for their husbands' well-being. They make excuses for their husbands' behavior and forgive the violent outbursts.

It seems to me that Dorn is not as far from Walker as it may appear. Both groups of women are caught in battering relationships because of their belief systems. Walker sees the women as believing they can stop their husband's violence by "acting better." Dorn sees them as believing they can change their husbands by being their saviors. Both groups of women fail to change the batterer. Both groups of women are deeply dependent and attached to their batterers. Dorn's women become victims by trying to be rescuers.[9] It is possible for a battered woman to fall into both Walker's and Dorn's descriptions.

The Profile of the Battering Couple

Those who have worked with battered women have listened to the women describe the men who battered them. At first, because so few men would consent to interviews or therapy, these descriptions were the only ones available of violent men. Recently, therapists who have been able to work with batterers have heard the men's stories. Basically their stories agree with the descriptions by battered women. From these interviews of both the battered women and their batterers, we can get a glimpse into the backgrounds of the couple and of their life together.

The information regarding the battered women comes from Lenore Walker's interviews with the women from the shelters and from Mildred Pagelow's questionnaire interviews of 109 women from shelters. Pagelow also reported on the work of two men who had worked with male batterers in couple therapy: Michael Wellins, a civilian employee of an Orange County police department in California who ran a crisis-intervention unit working with 110 couples, and Wayne Blackburn, a licensed clinical social worker at a family service organization who dealt with 150 couples who came in to get help for wife-abuse.[10] Other information on battering men came from Emerge, a Boston men's collective that works specifically with violent men in abusive relationships.[11]

The Childhood Homes of the Woman and Her Batterer

Walker found that although some women in her interviews had experienced or had seen battering in their families, for most of them this abuse from the husband was their first experience with battering. These women were raised in traditional homes where sex-role stereotyping was strong. The fathers of these women treated their daughters like "fragile dolls."[12] They were expected to grow up and marry a man who would care for them as their father had. They were not taught to care for themselves but to be dependent upon a man.

In Pagelow's study the women fell into two categories. The first group came from predominantly conservative, usually religious homes where divorce never, or rarely, occurred. Physical punishment was absent or very mild. The homes were either loving or very controlled, traditional, and paternalistic-authoritarian. The women reacted to the violence by their husbands with shock, embarrassment, and shame. They could not reveal the situation to their parents or families. The second group in Pagelow's study came from homes where violence was common. These women went from domination by father to domination by husband. They appeared to enter the relationship with some expectation of physical assault and believed that they had the endurance and the wits to overcome the problem.[13]

While most of the women did not come from violent homes, Walker reported (p. 38) that the batterers typically did. Either they saw their fathers beat their mothers, or they themselves were beaten. Even if overt violence was not reported, a general lack of respect for women and children was evident. Blackburn's experience was that *all* the men he had worked with came from violent homes, some of them extremely violent.[14]

Women reported to Walker that a battering incident would be triggered by a visit from the batterer's mother. The women described their batterers as having "unusual" and "ambivalent love-hate" relationships with their mothers. Many times the batterer would abuse his mother as well as his wife.[15] Blackburn reported that a wife's behavior that reminded the batterer of his mother could send him into a rage.[16] It would seem that the batterer was looking for that ideal mothering he never received as a child. He expected nurturing and caring from his wife. As one man put it:

> [She was] there to make me feel good. "Why didn't you fix my supper the way I wanted it?" That sort of thing. In any number of ways that was her primary role, I think, feeding me, nourishing me emotionally. And after a period of time, I became very inept at nourishing myself.[17]

The battered woman tries to fulfill her husband's expectations. She has so internalized the cultural myth that it is her responsibility to see that things go well at home that she thinks she is responsible for her batterer's behavior. She is not sure what she could have done better, but she certainly could have done *something*.

After we got married, every little thing would set him right off. It seemed he needed extra special loving at all times, and ... I wasn't doing that. Evidently, that was causing him to be very upset. I always got the impression that I wasn't loving enough, giving enough, that there was something defective in my character as far as giving love. That's basically the message he gave to me.[18]

Self-Esteem

Walker found (p. 32) that the battered woman has low self-esteem. The women interviewed devalued their abilities, especially their homemaking abilities. They evaluated their abilities connected with activities outside the home, if they had any, more realistically. The continual criticism from their batterers eroded their sense of self-worth, particularly in the role of wife.

Blackburn described the batterers as "men who adopt all the external trappings of an aggressive, controlling image but are dependent and out of control within."[19] Wellins described the batterers as lacking in ego-strength, with high role expectations for themselves and their families. Because they lack self-esteem, they try aggressive ways to maintain whatever self-esteem they have left. A batterer would say, "If I'm not worth anything and I want to maintain a relationship with you, I've got to do everything to try to control you, maintain you, corral you, because if I don't, then I'm going to lose you."[20]

Jealousy

Wellins describes the jealousy as pathological and coming from the batterers low ego-strength. The jealousy at first appeared to the woman receiving it as attentiveness and care, but then it grew to possessiveness and constant surveillance of her activities.[21] Walker quoted one woman who described it this way:

He used to drive me to work in the morning, pick me up at noon so we could have lunch together, and then pick me up

at five o'clock so that we could go home together. I couldn't
have any friends at work except those I could talk to between
the jobs I had to do during the day. . . . Bob was always there.
. . . I was accused of sleeping with this man [that she had
smiled at in the restaurant], and not only was I accused of
having an affair with him, but Bob spent hours telling me in
detail every single sexual act that we had done together. . . .
He also believed I was having an affair with my boss, and he
went so far as to call my boss's wife and tell her what he
suspected.[22]

Traditional Roles

Pagelow (p. 43) found a strong correlation between the
willingness of a woman to stay in a battering relationship
without retaliating and her strong commitment to traditional patriarchal ideology coupled with her willingness to
invest in her relationship with her husband. The battered
woman is a traditionalist in her orientation to marriage.
She believes that a woman's place is in the home. She
believes in family unity and the prescribed feminine sex-
role stereotype. No matter how important her career might
be to her, she is ready to give it up if it will make her
batterer happy. Walker reported one woman's story:

It was the greatest thing that had happened to me in a long
time. Can you imagine what an unattractive, intelligent
woman who thought herself asexual for so many years feels
when a man finally pays attention to her? . . . I didn't think of
myself as a woman. I thought of myself as a lawyer . . . but
when Larry came along . . . I found myself being the feminine
sweet little thing that my own self-image never said I was. . . .
I loved it. . . . I'm embarrassed to say it because it took me so
long and so hard to get to where I am professionally, and I'd
never give up my profession. I know that now, but there was
a little bit of time with Larry that I really thought I could.
That's how powerful sex was between us . . . there really
wasn't much else that was good.[23]

Those women who keep their jobs feel guilty. Many turn
the money they make over to their husbands. The battered

woman views the husband as the head of the family, even though she may be the one holding the family together economically.

Blackburn described his men as authoritarian and patriarchal. They are family men with very rigid ideas of masculinity and femininity and sex-segregated roles. When Wellins was asked if the men he dealt with were traditional, he replied:

> Yes, they are—they believe in segregated sex roles, divorce is unthinkable—but it goes even beyond. The difference is like people who can deal with lack of order as opposed to order; they have rigid boundaries . . . locked in . . . need for structure. Things are black or white, there's certainty, rigid expectations, rigid role models. This applies to both parties.[24]

Stress

Blackburn and Wellins both observed that batterers do not deal effectively with stress. Because they are men who must live and work within clearly defined boundaries with clear rules and parameters, one can see why a batterer would have trouble if things are not going as he expects. He tends to use primitive defense mechanisms such as denial, projection, and aggression to deal with emotional difficulties. Because he believes he has a right to beat his wife, he takes out his anger and frustration on her by projecting his difficulties onto her. If a batterer is a user of drugs and alcohol in an attempt to alleviate stress, that gives him a reason, but not an excuse, for beating his wife.

The battered wife's stress comes from living in an environment where she fears she will be beaten and feels she can do nothing to prevent it. The battered woman is a keeper of the peace. She expends enormous amounts of energy controlling the environment so he "won't get mad or upset." She controls parents, children, and events, becoming an expert at manipulation. Walker reports one woman's story:

> I would come home, and the kids would be waiting outside for me, telling me, "Don't go in, Mother, he's drunk and crazy

again, Just don't go in the house." . . . I tried to be better,
being good, being quiet, being very solicitous, being sexually
attractive, being not sexually attractive, keeping the kids
quiet, sending the kids away, but it never did any good.[25]

The battered woman has severe physical reactions as a
result of living under stress and fear. She may complain to
her doctor about fatigue, backache, headaches, depression,
and anxiety. The stress affects all aspects of the woman's
life.

Blame and Guilt

The batterer blames his wife for his actions. Walker
related an incident that occurred in a supermarket.

> The woman removed an item from the shelf. The man glared
> at her and said, "Now you've done it. Now you've done it.
> You've made me mad. If you don't put that back, you will
> make me even madder. Do you know how mad you are
> making me? Now you've gone and done it!" She turned to
> him and said quietly, "We need this for dinner." He looked
> at her with fury and said, "You've made me mad. Now you've
> really made me mad by saying that. You can just forget about
> your hairdresser's appointment. I can't stand it when you
> make me mad this way!"[26]

In working with battering men in groups, the Emerge
Collective, observed in the beginning sessions that there is
a high degree of defensiveness and blaming of wives for
behavior.

> I'm not trying to justify my actions or nothing, it's just that
> sometimes a man can only take so much. My wife just never
> lets up, I mean she really knows how to get me going. Don't
> you think sometimes the woman is asking for it?
> Yeah, and she knows just how to bust my balls. I mean,
> she's not big enough to hurt me physically or anything but
> she's good with words. She can talk circles around me. But
> what I want to know is, shouldn't she know how to handle
> me?[27]

Only when the batterer assumes responsibility for his actions
can the cycle be broken.

Sexual Relationship

Some women describe their husbands as gentle, attentive lovers at the beginning of their relationships. Then the sexual experience gradually becomes more abusive and sometimes bizarre. The batterer frequently uses sex as an act of aggression. Walker reports two stories:

> Peter was just the greatest lover I'd ever had. He was kind, gentle, and just, oh, so good. . . . But when Peter's mood changed, he could be the most vicious and violent man. I soon learned to be fearful until I knew which Peter would be with me.[28]

> I can't remember when we ever had sexual intercourse normally. I know we did at the beginning of our marriage but it sure changed later on.[29]

The Batterer's Dual Personality

The stories of the women Walker interviewed revealed what would appear to be a dual personality. The batterer would be congenial and happy, especially to the public, but in private with his spouse would resort to all forms of violence. He is charming and competent on one hand, and then goes into violent angry scenes with his wife.

> He's a good person, Walter is, not a bad person. He believes in giving to the public. He wouldn't hurt a soul. Why me? He pushes himself day and night to get his programs through. It's nonstop work all the time. . . . Sometimes I even like the glare of public life. Certainly it forces Walter to pay attention to me when others are around. But shut off the TV cameras and he's mean and nasty and ignores me as usual.[30]

> I must say that there were some moments on those camping weekends that were the nicest ones we ever had. When Jim would relax and feel good about himself, about me and the kids, life was just beautiful. You never knew, though, sometimes those wonderful moods could change just as fast as a storm could come up over the lake. All of us learned to recognize when his mood was changing from a happy, playful one into a mean, demanding, cruel one. At that time, though,

it was hard to get away from him, all six of us crammed into
that camper.[31]

Perhaps this dual personality is part of the "sanctity of the
family" notion. It is permissible to be angry, rude, and
violent at home but not in pubic. The batterer protects his
image to the public and the public believes him. Many
times he lies to friends and relatives about his behavior and
his wife's behavior, blaming her for the problems. The
family believes him instead of her.

Economics

As Walker listened to the stories of battered women, she
learned that the economic status of women in our society
works to trap a woman in the battering relationship through
her fear of deprivation or poverty if she leaves. Women in
a marriage are usually at an economic disadvantage. A
married woman in our society is usually dependent upon
her husband's salary for support. This is especially true for
an unemployed homemaker who has given herself to child-
rearing. The woman has few resources if she should want
to leave the marriage. She is unskilled for the job market.
She becomes dependent upon unenforceable alimony laws
for support. She may be deprived of child support because
she will not agree to visitation rights from a husband who
abuses her children.

In the marriage relationship, money can be used as a
coercive weapon. The batterer can withhold money as punishment. He can continually call into judgment the wife's
financial decisions. He may hand her his paycheck with the
order to pay all the bills, refusing to take into consideration
that there is not enough money to go around. If she tries to
cut corners by putting cheaper meals on the table, he
criticizes her and becomes angry because she is serving
inferior food. If she wants to work he may say, "No wife of
mine is going to work."

Middle-class women can become captives in their pala-
tial mansions when their abusive husbands control the

money. If they have been in long-term marriages without working, they may lack skills for supporting themselves in the style of life to which they have been accustomed. Some wives do not have access to the checkbook or to credit cards to give them financial resources to escape their violent relationships. One woman arrived at a shelter in the family's motor home without any money.

When a battered woman wants to leave her abusive husband, she faces the question of how to support herself and her children. The women who are most likely to leave are those supported by welfare. The more affluent women of the middle and upper classes are dependent upon a husband's support check. The economic power differential is very great if the husband has become economically successful and the wife has not developed the same economic power because she has been raising children. If the woman decides to leave the relationship or if the man uses divorce as the ultimate punishment for not living up to his expectations, the economic settlement in divorce becomes a real problem. The woman's fears of what he will do are deep, so she is easily coerced by him. The husband may threaten to take his wage-earning capacity out of the country to keep the wife from having the fruits of his labor.

Psychological Battering

Psychological battering accompanies physical battering and may also be present in a relationship without physical battering. The factor is still coercion of a woman without regard to her rights. The same dynamics of guilt and blame are at work. The husband can use money to control the wife by giving and withholding according to what he wants rather than negotiated transactions. The woman lives in fear that her husband will "do something." Walker relates the story of such a woman.

> "I'm really not sure why I am here," said Bonnie, while wringing her hands nervously during that first session. "I think it's important for you to know that I can't tell you who

I really am because I'm afraid that my husband will find out. I know you work with battered women and I'm sure I'm a battered woman even though he has never hit me, I just know he can," she said in a quivering voice. "I just know if I push him, he will."[32]

Possibilities for Therapy

Many battered women and their batterers have sought help through psychotherapy. Walker's evaluation was that the services of most helpers proved unsuccessful for the battering couple and detrimental to the woman. Many psychotherapists believe that victims often provoke attacks, so they do not deal with the acute battering incidents. They tend to treat the victim's symptoms of anxiety, depression, and other distresses rather than their cause, the battering incidents. Many women are given medications and even sent to mental institutions for the emotional problems caused by their victimization.

Traditional marriage therapy makes a basic assumption that the parties are equal in power as negotiations are made for behavioral contracts.[33] The batterer's resistance to assuming responsibility for his behavior and the wife's too-easy acceptance of the blame for his behavior are factors that make traditional marriage therapy unworkable. If there has been a history of battering, the wife is filled with fear. Her husband intimidates her into submission. She cannot deal with the hurt and anger she feels at being violated so many times. The counselor cannot protect her from a beating when she gets home because she has said the "wrong thing."

The power dynamic in a couple is very important. There are, as Murray Straus observes, "several reasons why even a single beating is important. . . . It often takes only one such event to fix the balance of power in a family for many years—perhaps for a lifetime."[34]

If the imbalance of power is not dealt with, the assumption that the woman is "asking for it" is prevalent. Wives often experience the counselor as blaming her for what happens. One woman reported to Walker:

> The marriage counselor seemed to be more on John's side than mine, but I thought that was OK. I really thought that if I could at least tell him all of these things that John was doing to me, he would tell John to stop, and John would listen to him then. But he didn't believe me. Each time I told him something that John did, that man would say to me, "What did you do to cause it?"[35]

A twenty-year-old daughter who was in family therapy commented on her father's behavior to Pagelow, "The worst thing about him is that he's so smart. We went to family counseling once and he drove the poor psychiatrist up the wall by sending the conversations around in circles as well as scaring him to death."[36]

Walker and a male colleague developed some fairly successful techniques that were effective in reducing the amount of violence in the battering relationship. In their view, the goal of therapy was to learn to recognize and control anger and violence rather than learn to "fight fair." The couple was encouraged to separate for an initial period of time. Each was to meet with a separate therapist so that each could gain some independence. Each person needed to be strengthened so that the relationship could become free of coercion. The goal was for each person in the couple to become interdependent, which meant that each *could* function on his or her own if desired. In the beginning of therapy the therapist carefully monitored the behaviors, structuring ways for the abuser to control anger and violence and communicate more accurately. As the abuser became more adept at handling his anger and communication, the therapist gave up control.[37]

Michael Wellins, who worked with 110 couples where the husband is a chronic abuser, limits his sessions to six weeks and then refers the couples to the Department of Mental Health, semipublic family organizations, or private counselors. He recommends assertion training, stress management, support groups for anger control, and *good* counseling.[38]

Blackburn has dealt with 150 cases in two years. He draws three conclusions in his work with the batterers. First, a batterer must be pressured into seeking help, usually when his wife threatens to leave. Second, the batterer tends to deny or minimize his violence and blames it on his wife. Third, the batterer will willingly continue in counseling as long as he can get his wife back home and keep her there. If she refuses to reconcile, he leaves counseling.

Blackburn insists that there be no violence as long as he is working with the couple. If there is violence, the woman must call the police and press charges. He feels that introspection is of little value because of the rigidity of the batterers, so he builds self-esteem, concentrating on interests where they excel. He recommends assertiveness training for both. He looks at the causes for stress and finds ways to remove stress and to cope with it. He works on alternatives for anger besides violence, such as time-out periods, calling a hot line, or hitting a punching bag in the garage.[39]

Albert Roberts reports on the services for batterers in the United States. In 1975 there were only two specially designed treatment programs for batterers. In January of 1981 there were about eighty.[40] These programs focus on changing the abusive behavior patterns with anger control techniques, behavioral approaches to stress management, and alternative communication skills. The goal is to help the batterer to understand the dynamics of his out-of-control behavior and to take responsibility for his actions.

One such service for batterers is the Emerge Collective. Emerge was formed in 1977 by eight men at the request of the women working in shelters for battered women in the Boston area. The need was to have counseling available for men who were abusive to their mates. Emerge decided to be an all-male organization working only with males, especially those desiring to overcome their violence toward women.

The men of Emerge have taken seriously the thesis of

Susan Brownmiller that all violent men serve to control all women, for the benefit of all men.[41] Emerge views all men on a continuum of violence and believes that almost every man is capable of violence at some time in his life. Emerge is committed to speaking out against violence toward women and making a choice to be nonviolent. Since violence is learned, they are discovering and teaching ways for men to learn not to be violent.

Emerge established itself as a collective with the belief that as men relating and sharing with each other they could help each other overcome the learned behavior of violence toward women. Their nurturing nonhierarchical structure served as a model for other men. Emerge sees the use of violence as a method of solving problems and settling differences as a result of three interrelated forces:

1. The socialization of boys to be aggressive and dominant in their social relations.
2. The reinforcement of these values by parents, teachers, and social forces such as the media, television, films, and the use of violence by the police and military.
3. The social norms of patriarchal society which dictate that men are the dominant gender and are free to exercise this power in family life, social relationships, and in the institutions which direct our lives.[42]

Males have been socialized to repress their feelings of fear with "big boys don't cry." Boys have been taught to be strong and to not display affection or other "female" characteristics. When men repress emotions, they transfer that part of their lives to women and so create a great dependency on women for fulfillment of the relationship. Woman's role is to second-guess her man's needs and meet them without his having to ask. The man's abuse is a way of forcing the woman to stay with him. If she leaves he has to face his dependency upon her, and that scares him.

Emerge has found group counseling to be the most effective way of working with men to change the patterns of violence. The peer-group setting makes it possible for the men to receive both confrontation regarding their behavior and support and models for change. The group also allows for a place to practice new behaviors.

Projecting blame onto the wife is a part of the early counseling sessions. By blaming the wives the men are able to remove themselves from accepting the responsibility for their own violence. They focus more on their own "good intentions" and on their wives' alleged "provocation" than on their own behavior.

In later sessions the men are able to talk about feelings and share with each other.

> I guess that's what men are supposed to think, you know, you always got to be on top of everything, but it's not right. I've always been a loner and I've never bothered other people with my problems, but sometimes you need a shoulder to cry on, not just bullshitting in a bar either.[43]

The men are by this time accepting more responsibility for their violence, looking into themselves and learning new ways of expression.

> As the group ends the abusive men are regarding their wives more as partners, rather than objects to be controlled. They talk about what it means to end the group and go their separate ways. They also make plans for their continued growth.[44]

Walker found that individual therapy has been helpful for the battered woman.[45] Psychoanalytic forms of therapy have not been found to resolve a battered woman's situation. Action-oriented therapy with a focus on moving toward changing behavior is more useful. Cognitive therapy to restructure her belief system is helpful to maintain change. Other therapies may be useful as the woman progresses, such as career counseling, assertiveness training, parent education, and some forms of couples therapy.

Feminist therapy has been most helpful for counseling battered women. Consciousness-raising as to the choices the woman has is the beginning. She will need to be aware of her situation. The battered woman has taken her identity from those around her, mostly males: her husband, her doctor, her lawyer, her pastor. The feminist concept of "naming" is helpful for the woman in restructuring her identity. She will need to challenge those who say who she is, especially her abusing husband, who has called her names and labeled her. Battered women's support groups draw on the feminist concept of sisterhood. It is in the community of other women that a woman's identity can be affirmed. Anger can be expressed and accepted. As the woman gets more in touch with her anger and what she has been victim to, her rage increases. The group can be a place where she can become aware of it and express it safely.

Support for battered women as individuals has mainly come through the shelter movement. The shelter provides a safe place where the woman can think through what she wants to do. When she enters the shelter, usually she has just suffered a beating. Most shelters have a 72-hour cooling-off time when the woman may make no outside contacts and can get herself together. She finds a supportive community in the other women in the shelter. She finds that she is not the only one who has been beaten. She discovers that there are some options and that she has some choices. Her whole outlook on life is changed when she is away from the control of her batterer and in a supportive community. Even if she goes back to him, which she may very likely do, she has been changed. She left once; she can leave again. The conditioning and experiences of a lifetime are not overcome and changed completely in thirty days, which is the longest time a woman can stay in most shelters.

Group therapy is offered in some shelters. Many times this is with a professional therapist or counselor-in-training. Other shelters are operated on a collective basis, and the women provide their own consciousness-raising and support groups. Some shelters provide support groups for women who have left the shelters. These groups have two phases. The first deals with the crisis of whether she will leave her husband, where she will live, how she will support herself. The second phase deals with living on her own, parenting, dating, and how to deal with her former battering husband.

Hot lines are available in many areas to offer support and information to women who are in battering relationships. It sometimes takes many contacts with supporters for a woman to gain enough ego-strength to do something about a battering relationship.

The recognition that the battered woman is truly a victim is necessary for us to understand and break the cycle of violence. Walker's insights into learned helplessness as it relates to the battered woman have become widely accepted as the basis of the battered woman syndrome. The future is hopeful as more effective ways of counseling are being developed to confront and eliminate violence inflicted upon wives by their husbands. The church can take advantage of these insights and practices to help the battered woman who comes for help for herself and her husband.

3
Theological Issues
Related to Battering

Theological beliefs become an integral part of one's being. These beliefs are very powerful for the Christian woman in a battering relationship. If a battered woman's religious convictions lead her to believe that the wife is subordinate to the husband, that marriage is an unalterable lifelong commitment, or that suffering is the lot of the faithful, then those convictions have the sanction of God. She does not want to oppose God so she obeys, stays, and suffers.

We have seen from the sociological and psychological perspectives that the patriarchal order and sexism provide an ideology that permits battering to "keep a woman in her place." Religion plays its role in supporting the patriarchal order and traditional ideology. The Dobashes, sociologists in the field of domestic violence, make this evaluation:

> The seeds of wife beating lie in the subordination of females and in their subjection to male authority and control. This relationship between women and men has been institutionalized in the structure of the patriarchal family and is supported by the economic and political institutions and by a belief system, *including a religious one,* that makes such relationships seem natural, morally just, and sacred. . . . Christianity, as well as most other religions, has provided the ideological and moral supports for patriarchal marriage, rationalized it, and actively taught men and women to fit into this form of marriage.[1]

The way one interprets the Bible, particularly in relation to women, is critical for a battered woman who already believes a patriarchal and sexist ideology. Using scripture to support the subordination of women just keeps her believing that those ideologies come from God. Views of God as only male, of suffering as virtuous, of forgiveness without justice, and of divorce as sin help to keep a battered woman in her abusive situation. We need to broaden our interpretation of scripture to recognize that the Bible uses many other images of God than just those that are male. We need to see that the Bible also speaks of healing for sufferers and forgiveness with repentance and reconciliation. We need to see that divorce can be an option to free for new life. These views can help to liberate a woman from the bondage of a battering relationship.

Biblical Interpretation

When one has a worldview of sexism and patriarchy as legitimate and "God's will," the lenses through which one interprets scripture convey the impression that the subordination of women has divine sanction and that scripture supports it. Although we are aware that the Bible comes to us out of a patriarchal context, it is the interpretation of certain texts for us today that presents a problem for women. It is the legitimizing of patriarchy by interpreting certain passages through the eyes of patriarchy that puts women under the rule of men.

A belief in the subordination of women is supported in the Old Testament by an interpretation of the Genesis 2 account of the creation story. Woman is created second as a "helpmeet" and therefore subordinate. The fall is blamed on Eve as temptress. The woman's punishment for this is subjection to her husband.

> To the woman God said,
> "I will greatly multiply your pain in childbearing;
>   in pain you shall bring forth children,
> yet your desire shall be for your husband,
>   and he shall rule over you."
>
> Genesis 3:16

The New Testament sanction for the subordination of women in marriage comes from passages attributed to Paul.

> Wives, be subject to your husbands, as to the Lord. For the husband is the head of the wife as Christ is the head of the church, his body, and is himself its Savior. As the church is subject to Christ, so let wives also be subject in everything to their husbands (Eph. 5:22–24).

These passages are not the only ones that relate to women and subordination, but they are the most important. Susan Brooks Thistlethwaite states that

> these verses were the undergirding of a patriarchal ideology holding as a matter of course that the subjection of women to their husbands was just and, indeed, sacred. In fact, the verses served to legitimate the patriarchal structures of the Palestinian family; yet their literal meaning has continued to be normative for the church.[2]

The biblical criticism that developed in the nineteenth century began to offer alternative interpretations to the literalistic biblicism. Elizabeth Cady Stanton took advantage of these new learnings. As an avowed feminist interested in the liberation of women, she had protested the inequality of women in civil, political, and religious institutions and had been referred to the Bible for an answer. Clergymen told the feminists that the Bible gave women freedoms but clearly marked out their sphere of action. Stanton challenged the oppressive teachings of the institutions of her day, including the church and its scripture. She gathered women scholars and the few women ministers of her day and, using the latest tools in biblical criticism, published *The Woman's Bible* in 1895. The work was rejected by the church because it challenged the belief that God intended woman to be subordinate. It was not accepted by some feminists, either, because of its radical nature. For fifty years it was out of print, but it was republished in 1972 and is available to women today. The publishers call it a "women's talmud," for it is an interpretive commentary on biblical passages having to do with women. *The Woman's Bible* stands as an important historic document, for it is the first major contribution of women to the interpretation of scripture that challenges the traditional view of the subordination of women. In the introduction to the Bible, Stanton states:

> From the inauguration of the movement for woman's emancipation the Bible has been used to hold her in the "divinely ordained sphere," prescribed in the Old and New Testaments. . . . How can woman's position be changed from that of a subordinate to an equal, without opposition, without the broadest of all the questions involved in her present degradation? For so far-reaching and momentous a reform as her complete independence, an entire revolution in all existing institutions is inevitable.[3]

The Woman's Bible took passages that had to do with women and commented on them. On Genesis chapter 1, the commentary states (p. 15):

> As to woman's subjection, on which both the canon and the civil law delight to dwell, it is important to note that equal dominion is given to woman over every living thing, but not one word is said giving man dominion over woman.

The commentary on Genesis chapter 2 (pp. 21–22) is a reversal of what had traditionally been taught:

> In v. 23 Adam proclaims the eternal oneness of the happy pair, "This is now bone of my bones and flesh of my flesh"; no hint of her subordination. How could men, admitting these words to be divine revelation, ever have preached the subjection of women! . . . The assertion of the supremacy of the woman in the marriage relation is contained in v. 24: "Therefore shall a man leave his father and his mother and shall cleave unto his wife." Nothing is said of the headship of man, but he is commanded to make her the head of the household, the home, a rule followed for centuries under the Matriarchate.

Phyllis Trible, a contemporary scholar, is restudying the passages used to support subordination of women. She explains her hermeneutic.

Within scripture, my topical clue is a text: the image of God male and female. To interpret this topic, my methodological clue is rhetorical criticism. Outside scripture, my hermeneutical clue is an issue: feminism as a critique of culture.[4]

Trible illustrates her methodology by working with one text, Genesis 1:27 (KJV):

> And God created humankind in his image;
> in the image of God created he him;
> male and female created he them.

The first task is to look at the context of the next. God created humankind on the sixth day after all the rest of creation. The account shows unique features in the making of humankind: only humankind is made in the image of God, only humankind is sexually designated male and female, only to humankind does God grant dominion over all the earth, and only to humankind does God speak directly in the first person.

Next Trible looks at the text in context. To adequately interpret Genesis 1:27 one must be sensitive to poetic language. Being aware of parallelism opens up new meanings. The text moves from a singular form for humanity, "he," to the plural, "them," specifically "male and female," which indicates sexual differentiation from the beginning. Trible concludes that *hā-'ādām* is not one single creature who is both male and female but rather two creatures, one male and one female. She also concludes that sexual differentiation does not mean hierarchy. As created simultaneously, neither male nor female has power over the other. Both are given equal power. She notices that even though the context identifies two responsibilities for humankind, it does not designate which sex should accomplish the tasks. There is implicit freedom.

Last, the text provides a topical clue for the study of the image of God. The metaphor of the image of God as "male and female" is part of a network of metaphors.

> For instance, metaphors such as God the father (Ps. 103:13), the husband (Hos. 2:16), the king (Ps. 98:6), and the warrior

(Exod. 15:3) are diverse and partial expressions of the image of God male. By the same token, metaphors such as God the pregnant woman (Isa. 42:14), the mother (Isa. 66:13), the midwife (Ps. 22:9), and the mistress (Ps. 123:2) are diverse and partial expressions of the image of God female.[5]

Trible observes that all these partial metaphors involve societal roles that the metaphor organizes but does not necessarily promote. The Bible overwhelmingly favors male images for deity. Trible reminds us that the basic metaphor in Genesis 1:27 of the image of God male *and* female challenges us to correct the imbalance and investigate the female images of God.

Trible traces the journey of a particular metaphor in the traditions of Israel. She focuses on one tradition in Genesis chapters 2 and 3, which embodies male and female within the context of the goodness of creation. Male and female are created from one, "earth creature." The word translated "helper" (*'ēzer*), which has traditionally been understood to mean subordinate and inferior, Trible shows to mean more accurately, in Hebrew context, "companion."

> In the Hebrew scriptures, this word [*'ēzer*] often describes God as the superior who creates and saves Israel. . . . According to Yahweh God, what the earth creature needs is a companion, one who is neither subordinate nor superior; one who alleviates isolation through identity.[6]

Trible is showing us that by looking closely at scripture and comparing the meanings of the Hebrew words, we can uncover a truer meaning than has been taught by tradition.

Present-day feminists are reinterpreting scripture using tools currently available that give us insights into the culture and context of the biblical times. These women have a view that it is God's intention that men and women be partners together in an egalitarian relationship. The questions they ask of the biblical writers come from this perspective. For instance, Letha Scanzoni and Nancy Hardesty challenge the view of Ephesians 5 that stresses the wife's subordination as divine order. They point out that the emphasis of the passage is *mutual* subordination, in contrast to the patriarchal order of the day that made women absolutely subordinate. The model of Christ as "head" indicates a beginning origin, or source, rather than a hierarchichal domination. The sense is one of inter-relationship.[7]

Elisabeth Schüssler Fiorenza, in her book *In Memory of Her,* reconstructs women's history in early Christianity. She recognizes the Ephesians passage as part of a household code. The author of Ephesians is prescribing behavior for the Christians in a clearly patriarchal order that puts the wife in an inferior position. Fiorenza sees the author as modifying the patriarchal code by putting it in the context of Christian love. The husbands are commanded three times to love their wives. Jesus' commandment "love your neighbor as yourself" (Mark 12:31) is applied to the husband in the marriage relationship. Christ's self-giving love is held up as a model of love for the husband toward the wife. In this way patriarchal domination is radically questioned.[8]

Rosemary Ruether has another interpretation of the Ephesians passage. She thinks that trying to make this relationship of Christ and the church a model of marriage is "contrived."

> The author is caught midway between the Pauline eschato-logical vision of the Church and the reactionary direction of the household codes, which try to return the Christian Church to the models of historical patriarchy. The result is a contra-diction that, nevertheless, for two thousand years has been preached to Christian couples as though it were a possible model of real marriage. This has been done by a selective interpretation that makes the text primarily a model of benev-olent paternalism and female submission.[9]

These authors and scholars and others are continually contributing new information to help us see women's posi-tion and story in a new way. We need to be continually exposing ourselves to scholarship from a feminist perspec-tive so that we break the old perspectives of patriarchal and sexist bias.

Feminist theology is a dimension of liberation theology. Beginning in the Latin American context, liberation theology is theology done from the perspective of those who are powerless in society. This is in contrast to traditional theology, which is done from the perspective of the white middle-class male. The biblical traditions that are central to liberation theology are those of the slave people whom God called out of Egypt and the prophetic tradition of the Hebrews at the time of the exile. The prophets called into account those who were oppressing the poor. Liberation theology remembers the prophetic tradition of Jesus of Nazareth, who came "to preach good news to the poor . . . proclaim release to the captives and recovering of sight to the blind, to set at liberty those who are oppressed" (Luke 4:18).

Letty Russell builds her feminist theology upon liberation theology, which she defines as "an attempt to reflect upon the experience of oppression and our actions for the new creation of a more humane society." Her liberation theology interprets the search for salvation as "journey toward freedom, as a process of self-liberation in community with others in the light of hope in God's promise."[10]

For the battered woman the good news is that God does not intend for anyone to be oppressed, that there is hope in the future, and that there is support (community) in the journey toward freedom. This may be hard for her to believe, for she has been in bondage so long to the beliefs that she should be subordinate and that she deserves to be beaten.

The images that Russell uses are the biblical stories of the exodus and the resurrection. The exodus is the story of the slave people oppressed in Egypt being led to freedom by God. They become a new people. The journey is a process. Jesus is the model of the new humanity.

> It continues in the story of the One who came as a *representative of the new humanity* who points us toward the goal of God's liberating action. And it frees us to participate in becoming, ourselves, representatives of that new life in which

there will be neither oppressor nor oppressed, but only man and woman in the process of liberation.[11]

The vision of the new humanity is one of partnership, where women and men will serve each other and work together in mission to bring liberation to all. This is hard to do in a world where human structures are hierarchical. "Submission is in fact an element of sinfulness in which women refuse to accept their full created status as partners with men in the work of God's mission in the world."[12]

Thistlethwaite shows how the battered woman has the possibility for change in belief and then in action as she relates to Juan Luis Segundo's "hermeneutic circle." There are four elements to his circle:

> *Firstly,* there is our way of experiencing reality, which leads us to ideological suspicions. *Secondly,* there is the application of our ideological suspicions to the whole ideological super-structure in general and to theology in particular. *Thirdly,* there comes a new way of experiencing theological reality that leads us to exegetical suspicion, that is, to the suspicion that the prevailing interpretation of the Bible has not taken impor-tant pieces of data into account. *Fourthly,* we have our new hermeneutic, that is, our new way of interpreting the fountain head of our faith (i.e., Scripture) with the new elements at our disposal.[13]

A battered woman believes that the Bible says what she has been taught it says, that women are inferior and sub-ordinate to their husbands and that she must accept a life of pain as her lot. She may then, because of some experi-ence, question that belief. It may be when her husband starts beating one of the children, or it may be when she thinks she will be killed by his violence. It may be some influence from the outside—such as a friend's comment, an article on wife battering, or as I hope, a sermon on the subject—that prompts her to begin to question her belief.

Unfortunately, many women who question are told by their churches that to question subordination is rebellion and pride. Some women then stop questioning. Others continue in Segundo's circle and begin to question a biblical exegesis that uses power against them. They use the new information at their disposal to form a new hermeneutic and discover that the Bible does not support wife battering. They begin to see that the scriptures are more on their side than they had ever thought possible.

Thistlethwaite concludes the application of the battered wife to the hermeneutical circle.

> The painful process of entering the hermeneutical circle gives us access to the realization that the Bible is written from the perspective of the powerless. The chosen of God are a ragtag band of runaway slaves. God, by this identification with Israel, is revealed as one who sides with those who are out of power.[14]

The message of both the Old and New Testaments is that God cares for the downtrodden, the widows, the orphans. God passes judgment on those who oppress.

> "It is you who have devoured the vineyard,
>   the spoil of the poor is in your houses.
> What do you mean by crushing my people,
>   by grinding the face of the poor?"
> says the Lord GOD of hosts.
>   Isaiah 3:14–15

Jesus demonstrated God's love to the poor and outcast as he healed and empowered them to live new lives. Luke records him particularly reaching out to women in the stories of the healing of Peter's mother-in-law (Luke 4:38–39), the woman with the flow of blood (Luke 8:43–48), and the woman with the bent-over back (Luke 13:10–17). We see Jesus' care in his acceptance of the woman sinner who anointed his feet (Luke 7:36–50) and in his raising of the dead son of the widow of Nain (Luke 7:11–17).

As Jesus identified with the poor, so must we in the church do the same. We must reach out to establish justice for those who are in unjust situations. Battered women are in an unjust power situation, in which their husbands abuse them by exerting physical power to keep them "under control" or punishing them for not "keeping in line."

In using a new hermeneutic, we challenge both the writers of scripture and the exegesis. We look at the important role social relationships have had in shaping our previous biases. We look at the power structures and ask if justice is being done.

David Trembley tells a story that we hope will not be repeated. A battered woman somehow found courage to leave her husband, although her family and church advised against it. The church's words were, "It's your duty. A woman must bear the prime responsibility for keeping her family intact. Besides, who knows what God's will is in this matter? Perhaps God is using you as a witness to save your husband." The woman remarried and was very happy. A tragedy occurred where the woman was severely burned. The church members came to her in the hospital saying, in effect, "This is God's justice. We warned you not to get a divorce. Now you are suffering for your sin. But God still loves you, and we do too. If you'll only repent, everyone will be overjoyed to welcome you back to your home."[15]

We need to continue to examine our view of scripture to ensure that the lenses we wear do not distort the truth of God's message.

The Maleness of God

Mary Daly has criticized Christianity as a patriarchal religion contributing to the subordination and oppression of women. As she aptly puts it, "If God is male, then the male is God." Although most scholars would deny the male sexuality of God, it is very clear that the predominant images of God in Christian religion have been male, especially evident in the image of God as Father. Daly continues, "If God in 'his' heaven is a father ruling 'his' people, then it is in the 'nature' of things and according to divine plan and the order of the universe that society be male-dominated . . . the husband dominating his wife represents God 'himself.' "[16]

The sex-role stereotypes that are evident in patriarchy have resulted in a polarization of human qualities into "masculine" and "feminine."

> The image of the person in authority and the accepted under-
> standing of "his" role has corresponded to the eternal mas-
> culine stereotype, which implies hyper-rationality . . .
> "objectivity," aggressivity, the possession of dominating and
> manipulative attitudes toward persons and the environment,
> and the tendency to construct boundaries between the self . . .
> and "the Other."[17]

The batterer is able with this theology to justify his aggression toward his wife. His behavior is consistent with the dominant male stereotype.

Daly sees the "male" God acting in three ways to legitimate the status quo in which women are victimized. First, theologians assert the subordination of women to be God's will. Theologians throughout the centuries have done this even to the twentieth century with Barth, Bonhoeffer and Reinhold Niebuhr. Second, the male symbolism for God is used to describe human relationship to God. Daly quotes Gregory Baum in *Man Becoming* (1970; p. 195) to illustrate.

> To believe that God is Father is to become aware of oneself
> not as a stranger, not as an outsider or an alienated person,
> but as a son who belongs or a person appointed to a marvel-
> ous destiny, which he shares with the whole community. To
> believe that God is Father means to be able to say "we" in
> regard to all men.

How does woman "share" with the community in this image? She does not belong. Daly responds to Baum.

> A woman whose consciousness has been aroused can say
> that such language makes her aware of herself as a stranger,
> as an outsider, as an alienated person, not as a daughter
> who belongs or who is appointed to a marvelous destiny.
> She cannot belong to *this* without assenting to her own
> lobotomy.[18]

Third, Daly asserts that even when the language about God is nonsexist, the situation is oppressive. The implication is that there is no problem of sexism. It encourages detachment from the reality of struggle against the oppressive structures.

Daly has an alternative for the patriarchal male God. She does not want to put a name on God, to "objectify" God. In contrast, she says (p. 32), "the God who is power of being acts as a moral power summoning women and men to act out of our deepest hope and to become who we can be."

Women being in the image of a God who is "Be-ing" then are free to become what they can be. They no longer are tied to sex-role stereotypes. Confronting their own being can be very scary when they have been accustomed to prescribed roles. Battered women breaking out of roles and into their own being confront something new and revolutionary.

Daly is aware that the breaking out cannot happen on an individual basis without the support of the community. "The burst of anger and creativity made possible in the presence of one's sisters is an experience of becoming whole, of overcoming the division within the self that makes nothingness block the dynamism of being."[19]

Daly has seen the male incarnation of God in the male Jesus being used for the oppression of women. Some ministers and priests still use the unique male incarnation as a place to begin for arguments for male supremacy. Daly proposes a new image:

> Exclusively masculine symbols for the ideal of "incarnation" or for the ideal of the human search for fulfillment will not do. . . . No adequate models can be taken from the past. . . . The point is not to deny that a revelatory event took place in the encounter with the person Jesus. Rather, it is to affirm that the creative presence of the Verb can be revealed at every historical moment, in every person and culture.[20]

Other feminist theologians are recognizing the destructiveness of the totally masculine images of God to females. However, in contrast to Daly they see redemptive values to scripture and are finding feminine images in the biblical literature.

Sallie McFague warns us that to absolutize any one image of God is to be idolatrous. She points out that the images and metaphors we have are very important. If our metaphors of God are not consistent with our reality, they become meaningless. For instance, if a battered woman has been abused by her father as a child, as many have, her image of God as Father will strike terror rather than comfort. The metaphor of God as Father that Jesus used was a radical one in his day. "Abba" was a term of endearment that meant closeness in relationship. The meaning of the metaphor of Father is a close loving relationship, expressing caring, nearness, and comfort.

McFague challenges us to seek new metaphors that will bring fresh meaning and will be inclusive. She sees parental models, whether maternal or paternal, as insufficient. She offers the metaphor of God as "friend." The image is found in the Bible: "But, you, Israel, my servant, Jacob, who I have chosen, the offspring of Abraham, my friend" (Isa. 41:8). Jesus is portrayed as "friend of sinners" (Matt. 11:19; Luke 7:34), and as one who lays down his life for his friends (John 15:13). God as friend is one who stands alongside, one who shares in the suffering, one who empowers. For the battered woman, God as friend can be one who stands alongside as she "becomes." The categories of subordination are broken, for friends are not subordinate.[21]

The image of God as exclusively male needs to be broadened to include more liberating images that will free a battered woman from her oppressive situation. The liberating aspects of Jesus and his ministry can be claimed to help in this process.

The Son as Suffering Servant

A theological teaching that works to support a woman staying in a battering relationship and continuing to tolerate and accept abuse from her partner is that of the view of

Jesus the Son as a suffering servant. If Jesus is our model, then we too will be suffering servants. Some biblical passages used to support this view are:

> "And being found in human form he humbled himself and became obedient unto death, even death on a cross (Phil. 2:8).
> "Although he was a Son, he learned obedience through what he suffered (Heb. 5:8).
> "For one is approved if, mindful of God, he endures pain while suffering unjustly. For what credit is it, if when you do wrong and are beaten for it you take it patiently? But if when you do right and suffer for it you take it patiently, you have God's approval. For to this you have been called, because Christ also suffered for you, leaving you an example, that you should follow in his steps (1 Peter 2:19–21).
> "Likewise you wives, be submissive to your husbands, so that some, though they do not obey the word, may be won without a word by the behavior of their wives, when they see your reverent and chaste behavior" (1 Peter 3:1).

John Calvin expressed this traditional belief in a letter regarding a woman asking pastoral advice in an abusive marriage. He admonished her to stay and "bear with patience the cross which God has seen fit to place upon her; and meanwhile not to deviate from the duty which she has before God to please her husband, but to be faithful whatever happens."[22]

Reinhold Niebuhr, among other twentieth-century theologians, has an ideal that comes out of the image of Jesus as self-sacrificing servant. As Valerie Saiving sees it, they identify sin with

> self-assertion and love with selflessness. . . . Love, according to these theologians, is completely self-giving, taking no thought for its own interests but seeking only the good of the other. Love makes no value judgments concerning the other's worth; it demands neither merit in the other nor recompense

for itself, but gives itself freely, fully, and without calculation. Love is unconditional forgiveness; concerning the one to whom it is given, it beareth all things, believeth all things, hopeth all things, endureth all things.[23]

The battered woman believes Niebuhr's theology. She believes the promises of her batterer to reform. She thinks if she keeps trying she can be good for him.

Mary Daly writes about the sacrificial love in terms of scapegoat psychology.

> The qualities that Christianity *idealizes,* especially for women, are also those of a victim: sacrificial love, passive acceptance of suffering, humility, meekness, etc. Since these are the qualities idealized in Jesus "who died for our sins," his functioning as a model reinforces the scapegoat syndrome for women. Given the victimized situation of the female in sexist society, these "virtues" are hardly the qualities that women should be encouraged to have.[24]

Evil cannot be owned as one's own, so it is projected onto the scapegoat. The battered woman takes the evil of her husband as he projects his inability to handle his own inner stress onto her in the form of beatings.

Jesus' self-giving love was from a position of power, as male and as rabbi, and not from a position of subordination. As rabbi, he challenged the male religious leadership. He confronted them with their injustices.

> But woe to you Pharisees! for you tithe mint and rue and every herb, and neglect justice and the love of God; these you ought to have done, without neglecting the others. . . . Woe to you lawyers also! for you load men with burdens hard to bear, and you yourselves do not touch the burdens with one of your fingers (Luke 11:42,46).

Jesus' message to those in power was to be servant. In answer to a question on greatness (Luke 22:24–27), he reminded the disciples that the kings of the Gentiles exercise lordship over their subjects. For Jesus, the greatest in the kingdom was to be servant. He gave himself as model of one who serves.

Jesus' ministry to the outcast was to lift them up to be whole. He announced it in Nazareth (Luke 4:18–19). He demonstrated it by his healing of women, servants, children, lepers, the infirm, and the poor, persons considered by society as lacking God's blessing.

The words of Peter regarding suffering were intended to encourage a persecuted church to endure faithfully in spite of suffering. They were not meant to encourage women to endure beatings and abuse from their husbands. Why is it that some male pastors and counselors tell a woman to go home and suffer and not call to account the one who is causing the suffering, as Jesus did?

As we look at the life of Jesus as he related to women, we see him treating them with the same dignity as he treated men. We see him lifting them up to equal status. Jesus chose the woman at the well to be his evangelist (John 4). He affirmed the devotion of the woman who crashed the party given in his honor (Luke 7:36–50). We in the church need to follow the model of Jesus, lifting up the oppressed battered women and calling to account those who are abusing them.

Guilt, Forgiveness, Repentance, and Reconciliation

For a battered woman the issues of guilt, forgiveness, repentance, and reconciliation loom very large. The battered woman experiences guilt when she says "if only" or "I could have. . . ." She is quick to accept the responsibility for her batterer's behavior. So many times she is told by her pastor that she should go home and forgive her abusive husband. If she desires to stay with her husband and work with him on their marriage, how does she forgive the beatings of several years, even though they have stopped? What is the meaning of forgiveness in her case? What does it mean for her husband to repent? If there are possibilities to build a marriage on the basis of nonviolence, what is the meaning of reconciliation?

Sue Dunfee addresses the issue of guilt in an article challenging Reinhold Niebuhr's view of sin as pride. Dunfee

sees the sin of hiding as the primary form of sin for woman.
She takes it out from under the sin of pride and names it as
that of which woman is most guilty.

> Woman needs to assert that human sinfulness is not just the
> sin of pride, but is also the sin of hiding; that the God who
> judges human pride must also judge human hiding and pas-
> sivity, not by demanding a sacrifice of the self, but by becom-
> ing the forgiven self to affirm her full humanity through
> grasping and claiming her call to freedom.

The battered woman may be hiding what she could
become in a life of fear because of being beaten by her
husband. To change the relationship by leaving or insisting
that she will not be beaten any more is difficult. To move
out of hiding is not an easy thing to do. Dunfee continues:

> To confess her sin of hiding is a deeply threatening thing for
> any woman to do. We have believed for so long that feminin-
> ity and assertiveness cannot be held together, that we persist
> in hiding behind husbands/fathers/children/bosses, and in
> the busyness of being somebody's "something" rather than
> in the demanding task of becoming who we are.[25]

The battered woman may be told by her pastor, counselor, or well-meaning friends and relatives that she should
forgive her husband for beating her. In popular piety this
may mean going back as if nothing ever happened. She may
be reminded of Jesus' model of forgiveness from the cross
as he said, "Father, forgive them; for they know not what
they do" (Luke 23:34). She may also be reminded that Jesus
told us to forgive "seventy times seven" (Matt. 18:21–22).

Sometimes forgiveness is portrayed as going into one's
closet and going through a transaction with God to "forgive"
the offender. It is not necessary to make any contact with
the offending person. The forgiveness is an issue between
God and the forgiver.

This private view of forgiveness is one aspect of forgiveness where the battered woman can deal with her own guilt
feelings and be affirmed that she is an important person
made in the image of God. She can receive forgiveness for

her "sin of hiding" as she opens herself to being made into "a new creation" (2 Cor. 5:17). If she has left her batterer or sees no way of interacting with him, she will need to deal with her feelings of anger and guilt apart from him. This privatized aspect of forgiveness is a part of forgiveness, but only a part.

This dealing with forgiveness by the battered woman cannot be rushed. She must reshape herself from one who has been devalued to one who has value in the sight of God. This takes time and the support of community.

For the battered woman, forgiveness is going from a state of having the experience of being battered control her life to a whole new stance of being able to move on to new experiences. Marie Fortune suggests a new vision.

> I will no longer allow this experience to dominate my life. I will not let it continue to make me feel bad about myself. I will not let it limit my ability to love and trust others in my life. I will not let my memory of the experience continue to victimize and control me.[26]

Forgiveness means recognizing that the batterer is human and that both he and she are made in the image of God. Forgiveness does not mean condoning his behavior or excusing it, but it does mean being able to accept God's gift of the future possibilities in spite of what has happened.

A complete view of forgiveness takes into account the dynamic of repentance. A look at the meaning of forgiveness and repentance in the Bible may help us to reframe our theology.

> Forgiveness is throughout conditional upon repentance, a word which quite clearly in its OT and NT equivalents involves a change of mind and intention. . . . For Jesus Christ, and therefore for the Christian, there is no limit to forgiveness, assuming always that there is true repentance on the part of the forgiven one.[27]

For forgiveness to be complete, then, there must be confession and repentance on the part of the offender. Batterers have a tendency to minimize and deny the dam-

age they have done to their women. It is necessary for the
damage to be confronted and confessed for repentance to
begin. Repentance means making the wrong right. It means
doing whatever is necessary to change.

Alan Richardson helps us with some biblical meanings
of repentance. In the Old Testament the idea of repentance
is expressed by the words *turn* or *return*. " 'Turning' means
much more than a mere change of mind, though it includes
this; it represents a reorientation of one's whole life and
personality, which includes the adoption of a new ethical
line of conduct, a forsaking of sin and a turning to
righteousness." The New Testament echoes this emphasis.
" 'Repent' in its NT usage implies much more than a mere
'change of mind'; it involves a whole reorientation of the
personality, a 'conversion.' "[28]

The model for Matthew's New Testament community
was to deal with offenses of individuals in the community
of faith; to confront and to judge and bring reconciliation.
If the offender was not willing to deal with the offense, that
one was cast out of the community.

> If your brother sins against you, go and tell him his fault,
> between you and him alone. If he listens to you, you have
> gained your brother. But if he does not listen, take one or two
> others along with you, that every word may be confirmed by
> the evidence of two or three witnesses. If he refuses to listen
> to them, tell it to the church; and if he refuses to listen even
> to the church, let him be to you as a Gentile and a tax
> collector (Matt. 18:15–17).

In relating this to the battered woman and her husband,
we see first of all that for repentance to occur there must be
a change of mind on the part of both. For the woman it is
the sin of hiding. For the man it is perhaps the sin of pride
and acknowledging the reality of his behavior. The change
of mind must result in a change of life. This means more
than good intentions. It means definite changes in behavior.

A complete understanding of reconciliation will include
justice. According to Marie Fortune, reconciliation includes
a concept of justice. Reconciliation means

to renew a broken relationship on new terms, and to heal the injury of broken trust which has resulted from an offense inflicted by one person on another. If justice is the right relation between persons, then reconciliation is the making of justice where there was injustice.[29]

For the battered woman it will mean the recognition of her rights to freedom from fear of a beating.

David Augsburger works with forgiveness, repentance, and reconciliation. His statements are very helpful in summarizing these concepts:

> Forgiveness is a brother-brother, sister-sister process, a two-way mutual interaction of resolving differences and re-creating relationships between persons of equal worth. . . .
>
> Repentance is owning what was in full acknowledgment of the past and it is choosing what will be in open responsibility for one's behavior in the future. . . . In repentance past injuries are fully recognized, future intentions are truly genuine, and right relationships are now being expressed and experienced with each other.[30]

Augsburger puts forgiveness in the context of community. Confrontation and reconciliation take place there.

Vernon Johnson's dynamic of forgiveness includes a concept of restoration. Johnson works with alcoholics who have some of the same dynamics of batterers, denial and minimizing of the damage they do. Many batterers are also alcohol and drug abusers. Johnson has found that one of the most effective ways to deal with alcoholics is for the community, family, friends, and employer to confront the individual with his or her destructive behavior to encourage and even force the person to get help. A part of the forgiveness and reconciliation is for the alcoholic to pay for any damage done when in the alcoholic state.[31]

This principle can be remembered when dealing with the reconciliation of the batterer and his wife. Restoration may need to be a part of the reconciliation. A biblical model is given to us in the story of Zaccheus, who when he was converted said, "If I have defrauded any one of anything, I restore it fourfold" (Luke 19:8).

Marriage and Divorce

Battered women tend to believe strongly in the permanency of marriage. One of the reasons they stay in their battering relationships is that their religious beliefs support their staying by condemning divorce. As one woman testified, "We were brought up to believe that it was more of a sin to divorce than to do anything else. . . . That's what was instilled in us at church. Separation was just as bad. Unheard of."[32]

An important theological issue for battered women is the view of lifelong marriage as ordained by God. The Roman Catholic Church views marriage as a sacrament that must not be broken. The Protestant church has long had the ideal of "until death do us part," which has been repeated in the marriage vow. The conservative branch of the church would say, "Divorce is sin." It is only recently that the church anywhere has accepted divorced persons as legitimate members of the community. The theological beliefs reinforce the stigma that our culture as a whole places on divorce.

The view of marriage as an institution to be preserved at all costs is prevalent among some pastors who counsel battered women.

> Pastor Jim paused, choosing his words carefully. He knew this sort of thing went on—wife abuse—but he had never before encountered it personally. They hadn't taught it in seminary. "Claire," he said, "whatever you do, make sure you tell your lawyer that his job, and my job, is to save marriages."
>
> Claire was stunned. Had she not told him of all that had gone on for eighteen years of marriage? Did he need an entire blow-by-blow account of the hundreds of beatings through the years? Did he really think Claire was giving up this marriage too soon?
>
> Suddenly Claire felt something in addition to her aches and intense exhaustion.
>
> Guilt.[33]

This viewpoint makes it almost impossible for a woman to leave a marriage if she has that kind of religious commitment. Her tradition, her church, her pastor, and her family hold her there. She suffers incredible guilt if she goes against her tradition even if it is to save her life.

An alternative view to the saving of marriages is to remember Jesus' injunction, "The sabbath was made for humanity, not humanity for the sabbath" (Mark 2:27). The institutions ordained by God are made for our benefit. Marriage is for the mutual benefit and support of the members, not as an opportunity for the stronger to do violence to the weaker. We have numerous stories where Jesus went against the sabbath institution of his day to care for individuals who were being oppressed by it. He healed the man with the withered hand on the sabbath (Luke 6:6–11) and the bent-over woman (Luke 13:10–17). He broke a sabbath rule when he let his disciples pluck grain to eat on the sabbath (Luke 6:1–5).

Those who advocate the divine institution of lifelong marriage quote Jesus' words in the Gospels as authority.

"Have you not read that he who made them from the beginning made them male and female, and said, 'For this reason a man shall leave his father and mother and be joined to his wife, and the two shall become one'? So they are no longer two but one. What therefore God has joined together, let no man put asunder" (Matt. 19:4–6).

What needs to be considered in approaching the biblical texts is the specific context and also how the believing community, Israel and the church, has dealt with the issue of divorce throughout history.

Myrna and Robert Kysar investigated the biblical teachings on divorce and remarriage in the light of the best modern critical scholarship in an attempt to apply those teachings to the ministry of the church. The authors' biblical interpretation is shaped by the presuppositions of the culture in which the texts were written and the authors' own cultural presuppositions.

They found the Old Testament passages on divorce to indicate that divorce was a common practice in Hebrew society. The legislative passages sought to minimize the cruelty that resulted from divorce and provide guidelines for divorce to be done as humanely as possible. Nowhere is divorce prohibited.

The Kysars see parallels in the way both Jesus and Paul handle the issue of divorce.

> Both Paul and Jesus seem to view divorce as a violation of God's intention for marriage. Divorce and remarriage deny the spiritual union that God desires for husband and wife. However, both Paul and Jesus stress generally the fact of God's radical love and forgiveness. Both contend that where there is a violation of God's intention for marriage—where God's creation is distorted by human failure—there is sin, but sin that is pardoned by the love of God.[34]

The Matthew passage just quoted speaks to a situation where marriage was being treated lightly. A school of rabbis was interpreting Torah in such a way that a man could divorce his wife for such a thing as not salting his soup. Jesus' words were to emphasize marriage of commitment. The Kysars observe:

> The early Christians did not attempt to make the words of Jesus into absolute, inviolable law for their lives. They did not understand the word of Jesus to be binding upon them in every situation. Rather, they took that exhortation as a guide for their practice.[35]

Today we have a reversal of the situation of Jesus' day. Battered women have such a commitment to marriage that they feel they cannot leave even though their lives may be in danger. The Kysars advise us:

> Marriage was made for humans; not humans for marriage. Therefore, when marriage fails to enhance and further the total well-being of the humans involved, it must be dissolved. The injunction against divorce must not be enforced with a strictness that results in the destruction of human personality and potential.[36]

When we are encountering a battered woman in the church, perhaps we can follow the pattern of Jesus and Paul and consider the individual more than the institution. When a husband refuses to get help and stop battering, then a woman can be helped to see divorce as an option that will be accepted by God and the church.

Those who give pastoral care to battered women need to be aware of the theological beliefs that work to hold these women in their abusive situations. It is our job to challenge these beliefs and offer new beliefs that are liberating. We can use our theology to empower these women to new hope and new life.

4
The Role
of the Pastor

The church community has the potential to be of great help
to the battered woman. The church is one of the first places
she is likely to come for help in her situation, and the
pastor, as leader, has opportunities both directly and indi-
rectly to provide that help and support.

Most pastors serving in the church are male, although
more and more women are entering the field. The approach
of male and female pastors may be different in relation to
the battered woman. If you are a male pastor, you can be
an advocate and a support to the battered woman. You can
put her in contact with resources and with female counselors and role models. If you are a female pastor, you can be
a role model to a battered woman by your very presence.
You have the advantage as a woman, if your consciousness
is raised, of understanding some of the battered woman's
experience from the inside, from your own experience with
sexist attitudes.

Because the very nature of pastoring makes it difficult
and impractical in most cases to spend more than a very
few sessions in serious counseling with a parishioner, all
pastors will do better to recommend counselors and other
resources to the battered woman. You then can be in the
background maintaining contact and support as she struggles to make decisions for her life.

Self-Preparation of the Pastor

You have been influenced by sociological, psychological, and theological settings, and so your assumptions and ideologies have been shaped by those influences. These assumptions and beliefs need now to be examined and challenged to see how they affect your care of the battered woman.

Worldview

If you are white and male, you will need to be especially aware of the gap between you and the battered woman in terms of worldview.[1] You are a member of the dominant culture. Most theologies and psychologies are written by white male authors. It will be helpful to familiarize yourself with other points of view. If you are a female pastor, you may have trouble understanding the helplessness of some battered women, for you have made the system work for you to a greater degree. Your task will be one of empowering the battered woman to begin to make some decisions that will be helpful to her. Feminist theology and psychology and liberation theology can expand the perspective of both male and female pastors. (See readings in Bibliography.)

Sexism

As a pastor you need to be aware of the pervasiveness of sexism. Sexism is based on a belief in inherent male superiority and privilege and therefore of female inferiority and subordination. Our cultural conditioning that males are supposed to perform certain social tasks and fulfill certain roles and females other tasks and roles is based on sexism. Included in this sexism is the message that boys are better than girls. Males tend to have the leadership roles and females the support roles in the church, as elsewhere.

Patriarchy

As a pastor you need an increased awareness of the reality of patriarchy, of its long history and deep roots in our culture and of how it has been institutionalized in the church. Women have had to struggle to gain greater opportunity for ministry.[2]

Domestic violence

As a pastor you must become aware that domestic violence exists, even in the church, even among some of its most respected members and leaders. It is easy to think that just because a church may be white, middle-class, and suburban, violence does not exist. Battered women will be there. Many will be active members. Some of their husbands will be there also, and some of them will be leaders.

Resources

As a pastor you should become familiar with the shelter in your area and the services it offers. The local chapter of the National Organization for Women or local social service agencies can recommend the shelter organization. Many shelters have hot lines and offer training for hot-line volunteers. Many have persons who are willing to speak on the subject of wife abuse to church groups. Find out how the police force in your town deals with domestic violence. Locate lawyers and counselors (preferably women with raised consciousnesses) who have had experience with wife abuse. Shelter people should be able to help here. Familiarize yourself with laws that affect wives. For instance, it is against the law in most states for a man to assault his wife. (See Resources listed in the Bibliography.) Here is an illustration of how a pastor can locate resources.

The pastors of Centerville were gathered at their monthly ministerial meeting. Sam Johnson of Community Church shared his concern for a woman who had come to him for counsel on what to do about her husband beating her. This was his first direct contact with the problem of domestic violence, and he didn't know how to handle the situation. He had given the woman a few words of comfort and asked her to meet with him again.

The other ministers mentioned similar experiences. They discussed how they might learn more about domestic violence so they might help the women in their churches. Then Pastor Sue Jones mentioned the women's shelter in the area. Maybe they could get some information that would be helpful. Sue was commissioned to contact the shelter and bring back information to the group.

Sue phoned the hot line and reached the director of the center, Janet Thomas. Janet was delighted to hear that the ministers in the city were interested in learning more about the plight of battered women. She offered to speak to the ministerial association about the shelter and battered women in general.

Sue reported back, and the ministers enthusiastically arranged for Janet to come to speak. Janet told them about the work of the shelter and its support needs. She brought pamphlets and a list of resources and was able to provide information on area counselors and lawyers who had worked with battered women. The resource list also included legal aid and social services available to these women in need.

Sam Johnson listened intently to all the information he was receiving, keeping in mind his parishioner who was being battered. He was gaining a new perspective on her dilemma. He was beginning to get some handles on how he could help her. He also learned that another of his parishioners, Betty Brown, was a regular volunteer on the shelter hot line.

Consciousness-Raising for the Whole Church

As a pastor you can educate the congregation to the realities of domestic violence and by example create a climate where all women, including battered ones, will find refuge and a sense of belonging and support. Here are some specific suggestions.

Use women as worship leaders. Eliminate exclusive masculine language for God and include feminine or nonsexist images for God. Many available resources now give new words to old hymn tunes, litanies, prayers, and benedictions, providing alternatives to traditional worship responses. (See Worship Aids in the Bibliography.) These new images free worshipers to see new visions of being.

If your consciousness has been raised, the effect should show in your sermons. Keep the battered woman in mind as you prepare. She will be there as you preach about justice, freedom, violence, empowerment, and the image of God. Use illustrations that include women. If you have a sermon feedback group or persons who give input to your sermon preparation, be sure you include some women in the group.

Support observance of the week protesting domestic violence, the first week in October, by including articles on the subject in the church newsletter. Your sermon that week could include a reference to the issue of domestic violence. Your local newspaper should be able to provide illustrative material.

Bring speakers on the subject of wife abuse and domestic violence from the local college, seminary, or shelter to speak to youth groups, adult education classes, couples groups, singles groups, social groups, and women's groups in the church.

Have a seminar about domestic violence, dealing with the psychological and theological issues.

Encourage the use of gifts across the usual lines of sex-role stereotyping: have men care for infants and young children; choose a woman as chair of trustees.

Work toward shared ministry rather than hierarchical ministry. Do church staff relationships follow a chain of command or are they collegial? Are assignments based on talents and negotiated tasks or are tasks delegated "from on high"? Is the chairperson of a committee "in charge" or do all members accept responsibility for what happens in committee? Are decisions processed by those affected by them or determined by the one "in charge"?

Have workshops on conflict resolution, learning effective

nonviolent ways to resolve conflict. Demonstrate these ways in your work with committees and individuals.

Encourage the formation of young married parenting study groups, using such materials as *Parenting for Peace and Justice.*[3] These groups make it possible for parents who want an ideology other than patriarchy to explore their options and work together to build a family based on peace, justice, and equality.

In seminars with young people and singles on dating, lay out the realities of patriarchy and sexism and work toward valuing persons equally. Work toward nonviolent ways of conflict resolution in intimate relationships.

In premarital counseling of individuals or groups, raise the issue of violence to help couples be aware of the violence implicit in our culture and the violence that may have been in their childhood families. In the course of the sessions you have with the couple or couples, explore the following questions:

1. In helping partners get acquainted with each other's background, raise the subject of violence. Was there any physical violence in their families, any hitting, slapping, or spanking? Almost every person will have had some experience with spanking because it is so widely accepted in our culture. Ask people to reflect on what it was like, how being hit made them feel, and how they evaluate the action now.

2. How does each member of the couple regard the use of violence in their upcoming marriage? Is it acceptable as a last resort? Discuss the issue of the violation of rights. Does anyone have the right to invade another's body space by violence?

3. How does each regard sex-role expectations? Does each have the freedom to develop his or her gifts? Talk about what their role expectations were when they were growing up and whether each wants to fulfill them in this marriage. Have the couple talk about what each wants to do in life in terms of education, children, and career.

4. How does each deal with power? Is it used for support and nurture or selfishly, for coercion, to get one's own way?

Help couples learn how to increase justice and equality in their marriage. Teach them how regularly to renegotiate their marriage agreement (contract or covenant) to increase both justice and satisfaction in the relationship. The Intentional Marriage Method (IMM) of communicating is a helpful tool. It is a four-step exercise to help couples build a mutually satisfying relationship. In step one the man and woman face each other and say in turn what each appreciates about the other: "I appreciate in you . . ." In step two each names needs: "I need from you . . ." In step three the couple selects a shared need and plans action to meet that need. Step four is carrying out that plan of action and then evaluating it.[4]

5. How much is each able to take responsibility for his or her own feelings and actions and not assume responsibility for the other? Plan some communication exercises so the two can learn to express feelings to each other clearly. The IMM will help here.

6. How does each potential parent view the disciplining of children? Talk about how each was disciplined as a child. Give some information on recent child-rearing techniques.[5]

7. What plans do the couple have for building a community of support for themselves? Lay the groundwork for each couple's deliberately seeking out a community of faith in which to live. Stress the value of this support and the importance of asking for help when they are in crisis. Throughout this process, establish rapport with each couple so that they will feel free to come for help when they need it.

Outreach and Mission

Encourage groups in the church to support the shelter in your area by volunteering for the hot line, giving money, or donating goods or food that the shelter might need.

Encourage the formation of a committee or task force to educate the congregation and recruit volunteers for service.

Open the church facilities for use by such self-help groups as Alcoholics Anonymous, Alanon, Adult Children of Alcoholics, Parents Anonymous, and Batterers Anonymous.

Direct Support for Women

Encourage women's support groups of all kinds: study groups, personal growth groups, sharing groups, and exercise groups. When a woman comes with an idea for a group, encourage her to start one herself and invite friends. She may ask someone to share the leadership with her. Offer her support with publicity from the pulpit and space in the church newsletter.

Encourage interested women to plan retreats for women. Suggest a workshop on wife abuse. Suggest speakers who will have a message urging women to develop their gifts as they were given by God rather than exhorting obedience to a role ascribed by society or "by God."

If there is even one battered woman who needs it, consider starting a support group because there are probably several more ready to join her. Find a qualified woman with some experience with battered women to lead it, someone who has had leadership experience and some training in counseling skills. This person could be someone from a church lay counseling center. If no one in your church is qualified, use your shelter leadership to search for one. It is important to find a leader who has sensitivity to the theological issues Christian women will raise. A local pastoral counseling center may have such a person available.

Find persons who would be willing to take in a battered woman and her children on a short-term basis in case of emergency. You would use these homes only as a last resort if the woman could not get into a shelter or find other refuge. It is important to keep the locations of these emergency homes secret to protect both the hosts and the battered women, for many times husbands seek out their women and are violent with those attempting to help them.

Let's return to Pastor Sam Johnson. When Sam got back to church from the ministerial meeting, he called Betty Brown.

"Betty, at the ministerial meeting today we heard Janet Thomas from the shelter speak. I was pleased to learn that you volunteer for the hot line. That's a very important ministry."

"I'm glad you're interested in the shelter, Sam. I really believe in what they do there."

"I'm sure you do. And I have a specific reason for calling today. Someone in our church has come to me for help because her husband is beating her, and I wasn't sure what to do. Would you talk to her?"

"Well, yes, of course, but—"

"I would check with her first to be sure it was all right, but it seems to me you are especially well equipped to offer her some support."

"Sure, Sam, I'd be glad to."

At church the next Sunday, Sam saw the woman who had come to him with the battering problem and took her aside, where there was some privacy.

"Sarah, it's good to see you today. How are things going?"

"Pretty good right now, pastor."

"I'm glad to hear that. Since our last conversation, I've learned something about our local shelter. Did you know that Betty Brown, from our church, volunteers there and knows quite a lot about helping women in your situation? Would it be OK for me to give her your name? She could call and arrange a time to visit you."

"Well . . . she'd have to come during the day when my husband is at work. He doesn't like strangers around."

"I'll tell her. You can set a time that's best for you."

"That would be OK."

Sam gave Sarah's name and telephone number to Betty and spoke with her after the two women had met.

"How was your visit with Sarah?"

"Just fine, Sam. She was a little nervous at first, because she didn't know me. I told her what I did on the hot line and how it could help to have a friend to talk to. She told me a little about herself. She and her husband and the two kids have been here three years and she still feels lonely. Their families are several hundred miles away, and he's a workaholic and very tense. He has beaten her several times and it's getting worse. She's scared to death. He won't go for counseling, and she doesn't know what to do. She doesn't want to leave him. She did agree to see me again."

"That's a good start, Betty. I'm glad you made the contact. Maybe we can figure out some specific ways to help her."

"I'd like that, Sam. I'm not sure just how we can support Sarah through the church. One thing I do know. It's important for her to make her own decisions. On the hot line we suggest resources to women who call. Just what resources do we have at church?"

"Well, we have a young mothers' support group that meets one morning a week, with child care provided. There are some Bible study and personal growth classes. We have the married couples class. Is her husband at all interested in church?"

"Her husband is working so hard to get ahead, he just collapses on the weekend."

"Let's not forget him. Perhaps one of the couples in their age group might contact them."

"I'd hold up on that right now, Sam. We need to know how Sarah feels about it. I wouldn't want to antagonize her husband and make it even harder for her. But if he came to church, we'd have a good reason to contact him."

"Good thinking, Betty. Let's begin by working on some personal support. Keep on visiting her regularly and try to get her plugged in with other women."

"Right. And she may be open to other options.

There's an ongoing battered woman's support group at the center, and Green Street Counseling Center is offering assertion training. I'll see if she's interested."

"Good. But I've been thinking. Janet Thomas said there are many, many women who are being abused that we don't know about. Sarah was one who asked for help. What can we do about those others?"

"I've been thinking about that too. We need to get some more helpers trained to be aware of the problems of battered women. The shelter is going to start a new hot-line training program. I'd like to publicize it in the church newsletter. Maybe if we start talking about battered women, more of them might come forward for help."

"That sounds like a great idea. Would you write an announcement about the training class for the newsletter?"

"Sure."

"Wonderful. Let's get together next month and see where we go from there. Perhaps the next step is a follow-up article for the newsletter."

Counseling the Battered Woman

Much of the counseling done in the church setting is begun on an informal basis. It may be a conversation after church, or a class, or a committee meeting. A woman may ask for advice on how to handle a tough home situation. You might invite her into your office to discuss the situation more thoroughly. If the problem is marital, you can ask if her husband has ever hit her, although she may not admit to you that she has been battered. If the problem is with the children, you can ask about violence toward them and then question violence toward her. Express your concern about the violence and the seriousness of it. Offer help in the form of resources and referral.

Referral is best for the battered woman, for she needs specialized help that most pastors are not trained to give.[6]

A woman basically has two choices, to stay in the relationship or leave it. If she decides to leave, she will need a lawyer who has had experience dealing with domestic violence cases. She may need a counselor—ideally, a woman with a raised consciousness and experience in dealing with battered women—but she may not even be aware that such people exist. She may need some career counseling. If the woman chooses to stay in the relationship, the battering may or may not stop. She always has the choice to leave again. The batterer needs counseling with someone who has been trained in the field of domestic violence to help him acknowledge and control his violence. Couple therapy is not helpful until the violence has stopped. Then it must be with a counselor skilled in domestic violence to be able to deal with the psychological violence that has a tendency to continue. Even if the husband refuses counseling, the woman may want or need counseling for herself.

Your role as pastor is that of pastoral care, being a support person and advocate while the battered woman is getting specialized help. When you refer her to a specialist, ask her to call you to report on how the referral is working out, or follow up with a call of your own. Ask which she would prefer, for some women do not want anyone calling them at home for fear of what their husbands might do.

As pastor you need to stay in contact with the battered woman and help find or maintain a connection for her somewhere in the church. This may be done by recommending groups or classes or organizations in the church or by sending a laywoman from a pastoral care team[7] who is familiar with the situation of battered women. It is important to check with the woman before sending someone to call on her. Reassure her of the continued support of the church. Check with her to see how she is doing with the referral you gave her.

It may be necessary to counsel a battered woman individually in some instances. You may have been able to establish a relationship of trust so that she may be willing to share her story with you. Here are some guidelines:

1. Listen to the woman and understand her situation; uncover abuse; recognize panic and fear. Take seriously her assessment of a life-threatening situation and the potential danger to her from her husband's violence. Do not discount her fears that he may try to kill her if she leaves, or that if she stays she may end up dead.

2. Listen without assigning blame. Believe what the woman has to say. Hear her story. Beware of the temptation to think she is exaggerating. It is important for her to break the silence by describing what is happening to her. Telling you the story is embarrassing for her. She is not likely to exaggerate.

3. Confront her with the reality of the situation: she can't make him stop and neither can you. She can, however, declare that she will leave if he does it again, or that she will not come back until he gets help.

4. Encourage her to find a safe place for herself if she is in physical danger. Such a place could be the home of a friend or relative, a shelter, a motel, or a church-family refuge.

5. Offer the woman alternatives from which to choose. Her vision may be so clouded from a life of abuse that she may not be able to see her options. Some of these options may be individual counseling, career counseling, support groups, education, help for the batterer, separation, divorce, or legal aid or counsel.

6. Support her decisions and choice of action even though her movement may seem slow. Beware of your tendency to want to rescue the woman. It is imperative for her to make her own choices: whether to stay or to leave, and how to do it.

7. Help her discover and develop her own resources: money, friends, relatives, employment, stress reduction. Encourage her to make contact with the nearest shelter.

8. Confront what is happening to any children who are involved in this relationship. Are they being abused

by either her husband or her? Does she want this kind of future for them? Sometimes concern for the welfare of her children can motivate a woman to act. In many states there is a legal obligation to report any known child abuse.

9. Have it as your goal to transfer her as quickly as possible to a woman counselor or lay helper or women's group for the support she needs to deal with her situation.

10. Maintain contact by checking with her periodically to see how she is doing and offer more information on resources.

In counseling a battered woman it is important to help her cope with her feelings of guilt, anxiety, and anger. Lenore Walker has some helpful suggestions: Help her express *guilt* by having her recount the details of battering incidents in which she could not stop the battering being done to her. It is essential to confirm society's lack of adequate help for her, but at the same time be encouraging about the potential for change. Control of *anxiety* may be accomplished through relaxation training, hypnosis, or recommending that the battered woman join a health club so as to focus on positive body feelings. The one area over which the battered woman does have some control is her own body. She has usually developed a lack of body awareness in order not to feel the real pain of her battering. It is important for her to begin to build self-esteem and a sense of power through body exercise.

Encourage the battered woman to recognize and experience *anger* each time it occurs. The difference between feeling anger and expressing it must be clearly understood. It does no good to express her anger to her batterer; this usually just gets her another beating. She needs to be taught to feel her anger, control it, and utilize it to be assertive about what she wants to do with her life, with or without her batterer.[8]

In dealing with the grief of a battered woman, it is

important to remember that she has lost what "ought to have been" rather than what was. Her husband has been beating her and she has overlooked it, hoping the situation will become better. When she recognizes it will not become better, she gives up her dream of a certain kind of life with him. The grief process is coming to terms with what really was and making plans for a new life. Encourage her to tell her story and accept the greatness of her loss, and not discount it because "she really didn't have it." Support her in making plans for a new life. Keep asking her what she wants to do, recognizing that it is very scary to launch out into new ventures. The grief will be real whether she leaves the relationship or stays. In either case she will be dealing with the question, What will I do with my life if he never changes?[9]

Don Parkes had asked one of his new parishioners to head a children's subcommittee of the Christian Education Committee. A few days later she came to his office almost in tears.

"Barbara, what's the matter? how can I help?"

"Oh, pastor, I won't be able to chair the subcommittee. Ben just had a fit when I told him I was going to do it. I feel terrible about letting you down. I really wanted to take the job."

"I guess I can find someone else. But I'm more concerned about you. Tell me what happened." Don had noticed that Barbara was wearing a long-sleeved blouse, and it was a very hot day.

"Well, Ben came home late Friday night. He'd been drinking—he's been doing more of that lately. He was in a terrible mood, so I tried to cheer him up by telling him what I had been doing. I told him about the committee—and he got so angry! He said I had no right to take that job without getting his permission. That I didn't have time to do it. He was really in a rage."

"Did he hit you?"

"Well, yes, but he had been drinking, and I guess I should have waited for him to be in a better mood before I told him."

"Barbara, you are not responsible for his hitting you. Has he done it before?"

"Yes, sometimes, but only when he's been drinking. And he feels *so* badly afterward."

"How badly are you hurt?"

"I just have some bruises on my arms, where he punched me."

"Barbara, it looks as though you are being battered by your husband. I've been doing some studying about this lately. May I tell you some of the things I've learned?"

"I've heard about battered women, but I didn't think of myself as . . . yes, I'd like to know. Is there anything I can do to get Ben to stop?"

"This is something that happens to a lot of people, and I have some bad news and some good news. The bad news is that if nothing is done it tends to get worse. The good news is that it can be stopped if both of you get help. Do you think Ben would go for counseling?"

"He's not crazy about counselors, but I might get him to come with me to talk to you."

"That's a good beginning. Let me know what he says, either way."

Guidelines for Crisis Counseling

You may receive a call from a woman who has just been beaten and is in a crisis situation, asking for help. Here are some guidelines.

1. Do not go to the home when there is violence occurring. It is dangerous. Offer to call the police.

2. If the violence is over, ask how she is now. Does she need medical attention? Where are her children? When will the husband be coming back? Encourage her

to find a safe place for herself if she is in physical danger.

3. Does she want to leave? Where can she go? Explore the possibilities with her: parents, friends, church-family refuge, motel, shelter. If the shelter is the only option, give her the number for the shelter hot line.

4. Encourage her to make contact with the nearest shelter for support no matter what she may decide to do.

Guidelines for Couple Counseling

Because of the specialized training and awareness needed to counsel in a battering situation, it is best to refer the couple for couple counseling. It may be necessary for each partner to have individual counseling or group counseling separately, through agencies such as Batterers Anonymous for him and a battered woman's support group for her. If for some reason you are involved in short-term counseling, here are some guidelines.

1. Beware of buying into the excuses and seductions of the batterer. This is very easy to do, especially if he is one of your parishioners and highly respected.

2. Confront the violence, both physical and psychological. It cannot continue if the relationship is to be healed.

3. Help each to recognize and be responsible for his or her own anger. Move to constructive ways to deal with anger.

4. Ask about influences that may be contributing to the violent situation, such as alcohol, drugs, stress, or belief systems. Give names of resources, such as Alcoholics Anonymous, coping-with-stress classes, biofeedback, exercise classes and groups, and assertion training classes.

5. Help both partners set individual and joint goals for themselves.

6. Lift up images of justice for the couple to consider in making a new marriage contract. Does each have opportunity for career development? Does each have opportunity for individual free time? Does each contribute to household chores and child care? If this is the major task of the wife, is it valued? Does each have a say in how the money is spent?

7. Help them learn to express their feelings, hopes, dreams, and hurts to each other in nonviolent, straightforward ways. Suggest assertion training classes.

8. One or both members of the couple may want or need to have separate group or individual counseling. Be aware of these options and support and encourage this desire. Locate resources for the husband such as Batterers Anonymous and for the wife through the local women's shelter.

9. Help the couple develop relationships with others in the church so that they begin to establish a community for themselves.

Let's return to Pastor Don Parkes. Barbara had called the next day to say that Ben agreed to come in with her just once, and a time was arranged. Don went right to the point.

"Ben, I'm concerned about the violence that happened the other night when Barbara told you about her committee work."

"She had no right to take that job without my permission, pastor. And anyway, I had been drinking."

"Maybe she should have consulted you, but that is not an excuse for hitting her."

"Well . . . I guess not. But I'd been drinking, and I didn't really know what I was doing. I never hit her when I'm sober."

"So if you have been drinking, that gives you permission to hit?"

Ben was silent.

"Barbara, is it accurate to say that Ben only hits you when he has been drinking?"

"Yes."

"Ben, do you see this as a problem? Would you like to do something about it?"

"Yes, I would. I feel terrible when I hit her, but I get so angry I just can't seem to help myself."

"Ben, Barbara, there are several ways you could begin to work on this problem together. Let me explain, and you can go home and discuss what you would like to do.

"First, I have the names of several good counselors who have helped other couples like you. There is also a men's group called Batterers Anonymous—for you, Ben—and a support group at the shelter for battered women—for you, Barbara. And you might consider Alcoholics Anonymous for help with your drinking, Ben."

"Couldn't we just meet with you, pastor?"

"I feel complimented that you would ask me, Barbara, but unfortunately my responsibilities here at the church don't allow me to meet more than a few times with any one couple or person. It would be better for you both to have help as long as you need it from people experienced in dealing with spouse abuse. What I can do is plan with you what course of action would be best. I'll keep in touch to see how things are going and support you in any other way I can. There's another couple in the church that has gone for counseling. Maybe they would be willing to tell you about their experience."

"Well, I don't like airing our dirty linen in public. It's bad enough to talk to you, pastor. I don't want anyone else knowing."

"I can appreciate that, Ben. Why don't you and Barbara talk over what you'd like to do, and we'll get together next week.

"But just one thing before you go. The violence must

stop before you can build a better marriage, and I have a suggestion to help you make that happen. Ben, if you feel you are getting so angry that you might hit Barbara, leave the house for half an hour or so. And Barbara, if you think he is going to hit you and he doesn't leave, you leave instead."

Pastoral Care for Psychologically Abused Women

The pastor may encounter a woman who is a victim of psychological abuse by her husband. She may be significantly involved in lay ministry in the church. The church contributes to her growth and support. Her continued personal growth may precipitate a crisis in her relationship with her abuser if she begins to want to make changes in her life and relationship with him. It is important for the pastor to be able to suggest an adequate therapist for couples or individual counseling, or legal counseling in case of divorce. These counselors must be aware that the battered-wife syndrome exists in instances of long-term psychological abuse.

Marge made an appointment with her pastor, Al Walker. She and her husband, Morris, had been long-time parishioners active in the church. When she came into the office she looked pale and shaken.

"Pastor, I just don't know what to do. Morris has left without a word."

"Tell me about it."

"I just got a job last week at his encouragement, and when I came home from work Friday he was gone with his clothes. After twenty-seven years and three children! I just don't understand it. I called him at work, and he said he wasn't coming back. I feel so helpless, so worthless. What can I do? I hoped that once he had finished his MBA and got promoted, things would be better and we could have some time together. Now he's left without a word. I can't support myself doing clerical work. I was lucky to get that job in the first place—

I haven't worked full time since our first child was born. And he's got a good management job. It isn't fair! I don't want to be poor all my life, but what can I do?"

"Remember, Marge, that everything you and Morris built together in the past twenty-seven years is half yours. And he certainly has a responsibility to support you while you develop a career."

"But that takes time, and I don't even have money for a lawyer. How can I make the next house payment? I don't know anything about financial matters. Morris kept that all to himself. He didn't want me to know anything about it."

"Marge, you're in a real crisis situation now, when it's hard to see clearly. I would like to suggest a woman counselor I know who can help you through this period."

"I'm sure that would be helpful, but I can't afford expensive counseling. I don't know how I'm going to pay the bills."

"I would like to get in touch with Morris, if that's all right with you, and encourage him in his responsibility to support you in this transition."

"I'd appreciate that, Al. Anything you can do will help. He won't talk to me."

"OK. I'll see if I can talk to Morris. Let's make an appointment for you to come in again."

Al was able to talk with Morris, who was afraid Marge and Al would try to talk him into going back. Al respected his right to leave, but encouraged him to remember his responsibility to Marge and their teenage son, who still needed financial support. Al suggested a joint meeting to discuss the immediate financial situation and future financial arrangements. Morris was open to that. He just didn't want to talk about going back. He wanted to be free.

Further conversation with Marge revealed that the marriage had been one of neglect and verbal abuse on Morris's part. The verbal abuse had the effect of diminishing Marge's self-esteem. After some reflection, Marge was able to see that what she really lost when the marriage ended were her hopes for something better. Her other major loss was financial security. She was afraid she could not make it alone. She needed career counseling and emotional and financial support during her time of transition. Al's task was to use his influence with Morris to encourage him to cooperate in supporting Marge without costly and time-consuming court orders. He helped Marge get involved in a singles group and kept contact with her to see how she was progressing.

Pastoral Care for Batterers and Abusers

Lenore Walker has listed some characteristics that may help us identify a potential batterer:

1. Does a man report having been physically or psychologically abused as a child?
2. Was the man's mother battered by his father?
3. Has the man been known to display violence against other people?
4. Does he play with guns and use them to protect himself against other people?
5. Does he lose his temper frequently and more easily than seems necessary?
6. Does he commit acts of violence against objects and things rather than people?
7. Does he drink alcohol excessively?
8. Does he display an unusual amount of jealousy when his wife is not with him? Is he jealous of significant other people in her life?
9. Does he expect his wife to spend all her free time with him or to keep him informed of her whereabouts?
10. Does he become enraged when his wife does not listen to his advice?
11. Does he appear to have a dual personality?

12. Is there a sense of overkill in his cruelty or in his kindness?

13. Does his wife get a sense of fear when he becomes angry with her? Does *not* making him angry become an important part of her behavior?

14. Does he have rigid ideas of what people should do that are determined by male or female sex-role stereotypes?

15. Does the woman think or feel she is being battered? If so, the probability is high that she is a battered woman and should seek help immediately.[10]

Although the focus of this book has been on battered women, I want to say a few words about pastoral care of the men involved in the lives of the women we are concerned about. Most battered women do not want to leave their husbands. Most want the battering and abuse to stop. You, as pastor, will be in contact with many of these men, if they are active and attend church. Planning programs specifically to help men during this period in our cultural history of tremendous changes in roles will encourage the changes necessary for peaceful lives. Men need to be conscious of and learn to express their feelings in ways that are not abusive. Support groups, men's retreats, and men's study groups apart from women will help. Important subjects are intimacy, power, conflict resolution, role changes, and feelings. You can refer men to such organizations as Batterers Anonymous and to Alcoholics Anonymous if there is a drinking problem. If you are a male pastor you can be a role model to live out ways of relating to women other than by using power and coerciveness. You can acknowledge your own sexism and cultural conditioning and invite men to join you on a journey to a new way of living. If you are a female pastor you can also be a role model of the assertive woman in the way you relate to the men in your church.[11]

Dealing with Belief Systems

As was discussed in chapters 2 and 3, we are aware that the battered woman and her batterer are characterized by having rigid belief systems based on sex-role stereotypes. When these beliefs have the sanction of God, or so the couple thinks, these beliefs are even more powerful. As pastor, you have authority given by the church members to, in a sense, represent God. In relation to the battering couple, this authority can be used for challenging belief systems that keep the couple locked into their violent relationship.

One way to begin to effect a change is to offer alternative beliefs when you hear one that keeps a woman in bondage. Here are some suggestions on how to confront them directly.

I made a promise to God for better or worse when I married him.

"That promise was also made by him. Marriage is a partnership. If he is unwilling to work on a better relationship, perhaps God will free you from that vow."

Isn't divorce a sin?

"Marriage as an institution is supposed to be for the good of the people in it. God is more concerned about the persons involved in the marriage than in the marriage itself." Recall Jesus and the sabbath (Mark 2:23–28).

If I pray for him, won't God change him?

"God cannot change anyone who does not want to change. I will pray for courage for you to carry out whatever you decide to do."

If I leave him, I will be taking the children away from their father. They need their father.

"What the children need most of all is supportive parents. Living in this violence is diminishing you so that you cannot be an effective mother. His violence is destructive to the whole family. God's design is peace and wholeness."

Aren't we as Christians called to suffer? Isn't this my cross to bear?

"It is true that some Christians are called to suffer at certain times in history, usually when they are being persecuted in large groups. Women are not called to suffer at the hands of their husbands, especially now that we have laws to protect them and resources for them to be safe. God calls you to be free from bondage."

Doesn't God care about my suffering? How long do I have to put up with this abuse?

"God cares very much about your suffering and has provided ways out." Recall the story of the exodus, God freeing the slaves in Egypt.

If I leave I will be all alone.

"We as God's people will stand by you and support you. God has promised you new life through Christ" (2 Cor. 5:17).

By informing yourself of the situation of abused women and the resources available, you as pastor can be prepared to offer help and support to the battered woman in your church. You can educate the whole church to an awareness of her problem and encourage the church to reach out in help and support. And you can give direct help to the battered woman by encouraging support groups, referral to adequate professionals, and personal counseling.

The Exodus Journey

How long, O God, must I endure this bondage, this abuse?
Not long. I see your bondage. I feel your pain. I will lead you out. My people shall be free.
But God, I do not want to leave. I am afraid to leave. I have a nice home here. What about the children? It will be hard for them. We can't leave.
I will lead you out. I have a good place for you to go. I have a land flowing with milk and honey.
The passage is very difficult, very scary. I'm afraid I will drown.
I will hold back the waters. I will lead you.
How will I survive in this wilderness?
I will provide food and satisfy your thirst.
I do not know where I am going. I want to go back.
You must not turn back now. I will lead you. I will guide you.
I am afraid. At least there was some security back there in bondage.
I will lead you to a new place of freedom. I will guide you.
I am so alone. Who will care for me?
I have those along the way who will care for you and support you.
I'm afraid, but I will go on. I've gone too far to turn back now.
I will lead you. It won't be long now. You will be free.

*What's that I see on the horizon? A new land across the
river? A new place to be, to become? I have been
without a land for so long.*
That is the new place of freedom for you. I will lead
you. I will guide you. You are almost there. Keep
going.

Let us as pastors be "those along the way" as ministers
of care and support on this journey.

Notes

Introduction

1. Murray A. Straus, Richard J. Gelles, and Suzanne K. Steinmetz, *Behind Closed Doors: Violence in the American Family* (Doubleday & Co., Anchor Books, 1980), pp. 36–40.
2. Lenore E. Walker, *The Battered Woman* (Harper & Row, 1979), p. 19.
3. Diana Russell, *Rape in Marriage* (Macmillan Publishing Co., 1982), pp. 96–101.
4. Walker, *The Battered Woman*, pp. 20–30.
5. Straus and others, *Behind Closed Doors*, pp. 43, 44.
6. Walker, *The Battered Woman*, p. xv.
7. Letty Cottin Pogrebin, *Growing Up Free: Raising Your Child in the 80's* (Bantam Books, 1981), p. xi.
8. Ibid., p. x.
9. Ibid.

1: The Battered Woman in the Cultural Context

1. Del Martin, *Battered Wives* (Glide Publications, 1976).
2. Erin Pizzey, *Scream Quietly or the Neighbors Will Hear* (Enslow Publishers, 1977).
3. Lenore E. Walker, *The Battered Woman* (Harper & Row, 1979), pp. 18–23.
4. Mildred Daley Pagelow, *Woman-Battering: Victims and Their Experiences* (Sage Publications, 1981), p. 39.
5. Terry Davidson, "Wifebeating: A Recurring Phenomenon Throughout History," in Maria Roy, ed., *Battered Women: A Psychosociological Study of Domestic Violence* (Van Nostrand Reinhold Co., 1977), p. 5.

6. R. Emerson Dobash and Russell Dobash, *Violence Against Wives: A Case Against the Patriarchy* (Free Press, 1979), pp. 6, 7.

7. Pagelow, *Woman-Battering*, p. 16.

8. Terry Davidson, *Conjugal Crime: Understanding and Changing the Wifebeating Pattern* (Hawthorn Books, 1978), p. 225.

9. *To Have and to Hold*, a film about men who batter women from New Day Films, produced by Mark Lipman and Emerge, a men's counseling service on domestic violence.

10. John Stuart Mill, *The Subjection of Women* (1869), introduction by Wendell Robert Carr (MIT Press, 1970), as quoted by Davidson in "Wifebeating," p. 16.

11. Robert Calvert, "Criminal and Civil Liability in Husband-Wife Assaults," in Suzanne K. Steinmetz and Murray A. Straus, eds., *Violence in the Family* (Dodd, Mead & Co., 1974), p. 89.

12. Ibid., pp. 88, 89.

13. Straus and others, *Behind Closed Doors*, p. 46.

14. "The Real Paper," February 11, 1976, in Straus and others, *Behind Closed Doors*, p. 32.

15. Ann Jones, *Women Who Kill* (Fawcett, Columbine, 1981), pp. 13, 14.

16. Straus and others, *Behind Closed Doors*, p. 43. These reasons are listed in the introduction to this book.

17. Ibid., pp. 192, 193.

18. Ibid., p. 206.

19. Maria Roy, ed., *Battered Women* (see note 5), p. xi.

20. Straus and others, *Behind Closed Doors*, p. 8.

21. Ibid., pp. 13, 53–55.

22. Ibid., pp. 101–104, 109.

23. Ibid., pp. 175, 182–184.

24. Richard J. Gelles, *The Violent Home* (Sage Publications, 1974), p. 187.

25. Ibid., pp. 111–118.

26. Ibid., p. 78.

27. Pagelow, *Woman-Battering*, p. 16.

28. Ibid., p. 69.

29. James D. Bannon, "Law Enforcement Problems with Intrafamily Violence" (paper presented at the 1975 meeting of the American Bar Association, Montreal, Canada), quoted by Pagelow, p. 77.

30. Pagelow, *Woman-Battering*, p. 82.

31. Ibid., p. 70.

32. Davidson, *Conjugal Crime,* p. 207.
33. Straus and others, *Behind Closed Doors,* p. 242.

2: The Psychological Dimension of Battering

1. Lenore E. Walker, *The Battered Woman* (Harper & Row, 1979), pp. x–xii.
2. Ibid., p. xii (emphasis mine).
3. Lenore E. Walker, "Battered Women," in Annette M. Brodsky and Rachel Hare-Mustin, eds., *Women and Psychotherapy* (Guilford Press, 1980), p. 346.
4. Martin Seligman, *Helplessness: On Depression, Development and Death* (W. H. Freeman & Co., 1975).
5. Walker, *The Battered Woman,* pp. 46–52.
6. Ibid., p. 57.
7. Ibid., p. 66.
8. Connie Dorn, "The Missionary Position: The Role of Rescue Fantasies in Maintaining Abusive Relationships" (paper presented at the September 1980 meeting of the American Psychological Association, Montreal, Canada).
9. Cf. Muriel James and Dorothy Jongeward, *Born to Win: Transactional Analysis with Gestalt Experiments* (Addison-Wesley Publishing Co., 1973), p. 87. The Karpman triangle in Transactional Analysis illustrates a manipulative role where the Rescuer becomes the Victim.
10. Mildred Daley Pagelow, *Woman-Battering: Victims and Their Experiences* (Sage Publications, 1981), pp. 100–108.
11. David C. Adams and Andrew J. McCormick, "Men Unlearning Violence: A Group Approach Based on the Collective Model," in Maria Roy, ed., *The Abusive Partner: An Analysis of Domestic Battering* (Van Nostrand Reinhold Co., 1982).
12. Walker, *The Battered Woman,* p. 34.
13. Pagelow, *Woman-Battering,* pp. 60–61.
14. Ibid., p. 107.
15. Walker, *The Battered Woman,* p. 39.
16. Pagelow, *Woman-Battering,* p. 107.
17. Adams and McCormick, "Men Unlearning Violence," p. 178.
18. Walker, *The Battered Woman,* p. 34.
19. Pagelow, *Woman-Battering,* p. 107.
20. Ibid., p. 103.
21. Ibid.

22. Walker, *The Battered Woman,* p. 116.
23. Ibid., p. 114.
24. Pagelow, *Woman-Battering,* p. 102.
25. Walker, *The Battered Woman,* p. 88.
26. Ibid., p. 189.
27. Adams and McCormick, "Men Unlearning Violence," pp. 184–185.
28. Walker, *The Battered Woman,* p. 109.
29. Ibid., p. 122.
30. Ibid., p. 165.
31. Ibid., p. 156.
32. Ibid., p. 236.
33. William J. Lederer and Don D. Jackson, *The Mirages of Marriage* (W. W. Norton & Co., 1968).
34. Murray A. Straus, "Wife Beating: How Common and Why?" *Victimology,* vol. 2, nos 3, 4 (1977–1978), p. 446.
35. Walker, *The Battered Woman,* p. 65.
36. Pagelow, *Woman-Battering,* p. 58.
37. Walker, *The Battered Woman,* p. 65.
38. Pagelow, *Woman-Battering,* p. 103.
39. Ibid., p. 105.
40. Albert R. Roberts, "A National Survey of Services for Batterers," in Roy, ed., *The Abusive Partner,* p. 231.
41. Susan Brownmiller, *Against Our Will: Men, Women and Rape* (Bantam Books, 1976), p. 229.
42. Adams and McCormick, "Men Unlearning Violence," pp. 173, 176.
43. Ibid., pp. 187–188.
44. Ibid., p. 193.
45. Walker, "Battered Women," pp. 354, 355.

3: Theological Issues Related to Battering

1. R. Emerson Dobash and Russell Dobash, *Violence Against Wives: A Case Against the Patriarchy* (Free Press, 1979), pp. 34, 44 (emphasis mine).
2. Susan Brooks Thistlethwaite, "Battered Women and the Bible: From Subjection to Liberation," *Christianity and Crisis,* November 16, 1981, p. 309. See also her "Every Two Minutes: Battered Women and Feminist Interpretation" in Letty M. Russell, ed., *Feminist Interpretation of the Bible* (Westminster Press, 1985), pp. 96–107.

3. Elizabeth Cady Stanton, *The Woman's Bible,* 2 vols. (European Publication Co., 1895; reprint ed., Arno Press, 1972), pp. 7–9.

4. Phyllis Trible, *God and the Rhetoric of Sexuality* (Fortress Press, 1978), p. 23.

5. Ibid., p. 22.

6. Ibid., p. 90.

7. Letha Scanzoni and Nancy Hardesty, *All We're Meant to Be: A Biblical Approach to Women's Liberation* (Word Books, 1974), pp. 98–105.

8. Elisabeth Schüssler Fiorenza, *In Memory of Her: A Feminist Theological Reconstruction of Christian Origins* (Crossroad, 1983), pp. 266–270.

9. Rosemary Radford Ruether, *Sexism and God-Talk: Toward a Feminist Theology* (Beacon Press, 1983), pp. 141–142.

10. Letty M. Russell, *Human Liberation in a Feminist Perspective—A Theology* (Westminster Press, 1974), pp. 20, 21.

11. Ibid., p. 133.

12. Ibid., p. 144.

13. Juan Luis Segundo, *The Liberation of Theology* (Orbis Books, 1976), quoted in Thistlethwaite, "Battered Women and the Bible," p. 310.

14. Thistlethwaite, "Battered Women and the Bible," p. 311.

15. David Trembley, "Breaking the Silence: Wife Beating and the Churches," *Christianity and Crisis,* February 21, 1983, p. 39.

16. Mary Daly, *Beyond God the Father: Toward a Philosophy of Women's Liberation* (Beacon Press, 1973), pp. 19, 13.

17. Ibid., p. 15.

18. Ibid., p. 20.

19. Ibid., p. 41.

20. Ibid., p. 71.

21. Sallie McFague, *Metaphorical Theology: Models of God in Religious Language* (Fortress Press, 1982), pp. 3, 117.

22. Calvin, *Calvini Opera* 17, p. 539, trans. by Philip E. Hughes, ed., *The Register of the Company of Pastors of Geneva in the Time of Calvin* (Wm. B. Eerdmans Publishing Co., 1966), pp. 344–345, as quoted in Jane Dempsey Douglass, "Women and the Continental Reformation," in Rosemary Radford Ruether, ed., *Religion and Sexism* (Simon & Schuster, 1974), p, 301.

23. Valerie Saiving, "The Human Situation: A Feminine View,"

in Carol P. Christ and Judith Plaskow, eds., *Womanspirit Rising: A Feminist Reader in Religion* (Harper & Row, 1979), pp. 26–27.

24. Daly, *Beyond God the Father,* p. 77.

25. Sue Nelson Dunfee, "The Sin of Hiding: A Feminist Critique of Reinhold Niebuhr's Account of the Sin of Pride," *Soundings,* Fall 1982, pp. 317, 324.

26. Marie Marshall Fortune, *Sexual Violence; The Unmentionable Sin: An Ethical and Pastoral Perspective* (Pilgrim Press, 1983), p. 209.

27. Alan Richardson, ed., *A Theological Word Book of the Bible* (Macmillan Co., 1950), p. 86.

28. Ibid., pp. 191, 192.

29. Fortune, *Sexual Violence,* p. 213.

30. David Augsburger, *Caring Enough to Forgive: Caring Enough Not to Forgive* (Herald Press, 1981), pp. 34, 72.

31. Vernon E. Johnson, *I'll Quit Tomorrow: A Practical Guide to Alcoholism Treatment,* rev. ed. (Harper & Row, 1980), pp. 114–125.

32. Esther Lee Olson with Kenneth Petersen, *No Place to Hide; Wife Abuse: Anatomy of a Private Crime* (Tyndale House Publishers, 1982), p. 17.

33. Ibid., p. 96.

34. Myrna and Robert Kysar, *The Asundered: Biblical Teachings on Divorce and Remarriage* (John Knox Press, 1978), p. 83.

35. Ibid., p. 91.

36. Ibid., p. 92.

4: The Role of the Pastor

1. See Derald W. Sue and others, *Counseling the Culturally Different: Theory and Practice,* ch. 4, "Dimensions of World Views: Cultural Identity" (John Wiley & Sons, 1981).

2. Del Martin, *Battered Wives* (Glide Publications, 1976). A history of domestic violence in the context of sexism and patriarchy.

3. Kathleen and James McGinnis, *Parenting for Peace and Justice* (Orbis Books, 1981). A seven-week leader's guide with worksheets is also available. It includes an excellent chapter on sex-role stereotyping. Tapes, program guide, and filmstrip are available for families in churches exploring positive models of parenting and family life. Discipleship Resources, 1908 Grand Avenue, P.O. Box 189, Nashville, TN 37202.

4. Howard J. Clinebell, Jr., *Growth Counseling for Marriage Enrichment: Pre-Marriage and the Early Years* (Fortress Press, 1975), esp. ch. 2, "The Intentional Marriage Method—A Basic Growth Tool," and ch. 4, "Preparing for a Good Marriage."

5. Letty Cottin Pogrebin, *Growing Up Free* (Bantam Books, 1981). The National Center for the Study of Corporal Punishment and Alternatives in the Schools is committed to research, education, and advocacy. For information on materials, workshops, and services, write to 833 Ritter Annex, Temple University, Philadelphia, PA 19122. The following articles are helpful: Robert R. Gillogly, "Spanking Hurts Everybody," *Theology Today,* January 1981, pp. 415–424; Irwin A. Hyman and Dolores Lally, "Discipline in the 1980's: Some Alternatives to Corporal Punishment," *Children Today,* January–February 1982, pp. 10–13. Excellent quality books by Joy Berry are directed toward children with parent helps.

6. Howard W. Stone, *The Caring Church: A Guide for Lay Pastoral Care* (Harper & Row, 1983), pp. 89–93. Concrete suggestions for referral in general.

7. Ibid. This is an excellent guide for a lay training program. See also Diane Detwiler-Zapp and William Caveness Dixon, *Lay Caregiving* (Fortress Press, 1982).

8. Lenore E. Walker, *The Battered Woman* (Harper & Row, 1979), pp. 238, 239.

9. Wayne E. Oates, *Pastoral Care and Counseling in Grief and Separation* (Fortress Press, 1976); Phyllis R. Silverman, *Helping Women Cope with Grief* (Sage Publications, 1981), ch. 5, "The Grief of Battered Women."

10. Walker, *The Battered Woman,* p. 254, adapted.

11. Robert E. Alberti and Michael L. Emmons, *Your Perfect Right: A Guide to Assertive Living,* 4th ed. (Impact Publishers, 1982); David Augsburger, *Anger and Assertiveness in Pastoral Care* (Fortress Press, 1979); David Augsburger and John Faul, *Beyond Assertiveness* (Word Books, 1980); Seattle-King County NOW, *Woman, Assert Your Self! An Instructive Handbook* (Harper & Row, 1974).

Bibliography
and Resources

Feminist
and Liberation Readings

Chesler, Phyllis. *Women and Madness.* Avon Books, 1973. A critique on the negative effects of the psychotherapeutic field on women.

Christ, Carol P., and Judith Plaskow, eds. *Womanspirit Rising: A Feminist Reader in Religion.* Harper & Row, 1979. A collection of articles from feminist theologians and scholars.

Clinebell, Charlotte Holt. *Counseling for Liberation.* Fortress Press, 1976. Feminist perspectives in counseling.

Cone, James. *God of the Oppressed.* Seabury Press, 1975. A key work on black liberation theology.

Daly, Mary. *Beyond God the Father: Toward a Philosophy of Women's Liberation.* Beacon Press, 1973. A major work on radical feminism.

Fortune, Marie Marshall. *Sexual Violence: The Unmentionable Sin: An Ethical and Pastoral Perspective.* Pilgrim Press, 1983. Important discussion of this subject by an expert in the field.

Freire, Paulo. *Pedagogy of the Oppressed.* Continuum Publishing Co., 1970. A classic work from a South American perspective.

Gilbert, Lucia Albino. "Feminist Therapy." In Annette M. Brodsky and Rachel Hare-Mustin, eds., *Women and Psychotherapy.* Guilford Press, 1980, pp. 245–265.

Mander, Anica Vesel, and Anne Kent Rush. *Feminism as Therapy.* Bookworks/Random House, 1975. A constructive model of therapy.

Miller, Jean Baker. *Toward a New Psychology of Women.* Beacon Press, 1977. A look at the valuable contributions women make to society (nurture, care).

Morton, Nelle. *The Journey Is Home.* Beacon Press, 1985. A

powerful collection of the 1970s writings of this distinguished theologian on metaphor, image, and myth.

Russell, Letty M. *Human Liberation in a Feminist Perspective—A Theology.* Westminster Press, 1974. Feminism from a biblical and Reformed position.

Scanzoni, Letha, and Nancy Hardesty. *All We're Meant to Be: A Biblical Approach to Women's Liberation.* Word Books, 1974. A biblical feminist point of view.

Tennis, Diane. *Is God the Only Reliable Father?* Westminster Press, 1985. A rethinking of the image and relationship with God the Father.

Thistlethwaite, Susan Brooks. "Every Two Minutes: Battered Women and Feminist Interpretation." In Letty M. Russell, ed., *Feminist Interpretation of the Bible.* Westminster Press, 1985. The power of feminist interpretation to empower and free battered women.

Walker, Lenore E. *The Battered Woman.* Harper & Row, 1979. A major work from a feminist perspective.

Wilson-Schaef, Anne. *Women's Reality: An Emerging Female System in the White Male Society.* Winston Press, 1981. A description of women's reality as legitimate reality and option in dominant white male culture.

Resources

Organizations

Center for the Prevention of Sexual and Domestic Violence
1914 North 34th Street, Suite 205, Seattle, WA 98103
206–634–1903
Center for Women Policy Studies
2000 P Street, NW, Suite 508, Washington, DC 20036
202–872–1770
National Coalition Against Domestic Violence
1500 Massachusetts Avenue NW, Washington, DC 20005
202–347–7017

Manuals

Fortune, Marie, and Denise Hormann. *Family Violence: A Workshop Manual for Clergy and Other Service Providers.* Center for the Prevention of Sexual and Domestic Violence, 1980.

NiCarthy, Ginny. *Getting Free: A Handbook for Women in Abusive Relationships.* Seal Pr-Feminist, 1982.

Sonkin, Daniel J., and Michael Durphy. *Learning to Live Without Violence: A Handbook for Men.* Volcano Press, 1982.

Newsletters

Response to Violence in the Family and Sexual Assault. A bimonthly publication of the Center for Women Policy Studies. Information on medical, social service, legal, and legislative developments in the field of family violence.

Working Together. A quarterly publication of the Center for the Prevention of Sexual and Domestic Violence. Useful resource information for the church community.

Films

Battered Women: Violence Behind Closed Doors. A film produced by J. Gary Mitchell Film Company, Sausalito, CA, 1977. 16mm., color, 24 minutes. Battered women describe their feelings of helplessness, fear, and guilt. The film explores options for women and methods of intervention and counseling. Order from the Center for Women Policy Studies (202–872–1770).

Time Out. A series of three short films on spouse abuse, seen through the eyes of men. 16mm., color, 12 to 18 min. each. A discussion guide is available. Obtain through ODN Productions, 74 Varick Street, New York, NY 10013 (212–431–8923), *or* 1454 Sixth Street, Berkeley, CA 94701.

To Have and to Hold. A film about men who batter women. 16mm., color, 20 min. New Day Films, P.O. Box 315, Franklin Lakes, NJ 07417 (212–891–8240).

We Will Not Be Beaten. A film produced by women who have themselves been battered, telling their own stories. 16mm., black and white, 35 min. Transition House Films, 25 West Street, 5th floor, Boston, MA 02111.

Denominational Materials

Each denomination has materials on battered women and domestic violence. Explore and take advantage of the resources of your own denomination.

Other Counseling Resources

Ball, Patricia G., and Elizabeth Wyman. "Battered Wives and Powerlessness: What Can Counselors Do?" *Victimology,* vol. 2, nos. 3, 4 (1977–1978), pp. 545–552.

Fleming, Jennifer Baker. *Stopping Wife Abuse: A Guide to the Emotional, Psychological, and Legal Implications . . . for the Abused Woman and Those Helping Her.* Doubleday & Co., Anchor Books, 1979.

Franks, Violet, and Vasanti Burtle, eds. *Women in Therapy.* Brunner/Mazel, 1974.

Gilligan, Carol. *In a Different Voice: Psychological Theory and Woman's Development.* Harvard University Press, 1982.

Hare-Mustin, Rachel T. "A Feminist Approach to Family Therapy." *Family Process,* June 1978, pp. 181–194.

Lerman, Lisa G. *Legal Help for Battered Women.* Center for Women Policy Studies, 1981.

Norwood, Robin. *Women Who Love Too Much: When You Keep Wishing and Hoping He'll Change.* St. Martin's Press, 1985.

Rawlings, Edna I., and Dianne K. Carter, eds. *Psychotherapy for Women: Treatment Toward Equality.* Charles C Thomas, 1977.

Rice, David G., and Joy K. Rice. "Non-Sexist 'Marital' Therapy." *Journal of Marriage and Family Counseling,* January 1977, pp. 3–10.

Schechter, Susan. *Women and Male Violence: The Visions and Struggles of the Battered Women's Movement.* South End Press, 1982.

Silverman, Phyllis R. *Helping Women Cope with Grief.* Sage Publications, 1981. Ch. 5, "The Grief of Battered Women."

Worship Aids

Primary Resources

Watley, William D., ed. *The Word and Words: Beyond Gender in Theological and Liturgical Language.* Consultation on Church Union, 1983.

General Resources

Clark, Linda, Marian Ronan, and Eleanor Walker. *Image Breaking, Image Building: A Handbook for Creative Worship with Women of Christian Tradition.* Pilgrim Press, 1981.

Gjerding, Iben, and Katherine Kinnamon, eds. *No Longer Strangers: A Resource for Women and Worship.* World Council of Churches, 1983.

Hinton, Pat Corrick. *Images of Peace.* Winston Press, 1984.

Miller, Casey, and Kate Swift. *The Handbook of Nonsexist Writing.* Lippincott & Crowell, 1980.

Neufer Emswiler, Sharon, and Thomas Neufer Emswiler. *Women and Worship: A Guide to Nonsexist Hymns, Prayers, and Liturgies.* Rev. & exp. ed. Harper & Row, 1984.

Neufer Emswiler, Thomas, and Sharon Neufer Emswiler. *Wholeness in Worship: Creative Models for Sunday, Family, and Special Services.* Harper & Row, 1980.

Sawicki, Marianne. *Faith and Sexism: Guidelines for Religious Educators.* Seabury Press, 1979.

Watkins, Keith. *Faithful and Fair: Transcending Sexist Language in Worship.* Abingdon Press, 1981.

Weems, Ann. *Reaching for Rainbows: Resources for Creative Worship.* Westminster Press, 1980.

Withers, Barbara, ed. *Language About God in Liturgy and Scripture: A Study Guide.* Geneva Press, 1980.

―――. *Language and the Church: Articles and Designs for Workshops.* Division of Education and Ministry, National Council of the Churches of Christ in the U.S.A, 1984.

Lectionary Aids

Hessel, Dieter T., ed. *Social Themes of the Christian Year: A Commentary on the Lectionary.* Geneva Press, 1983.

An Inclusive Language Lectionary: Readings for Year A. National Council of the Churches of Christ in the U.S.A. John Knox Press, Pilgrim Press, Westminster Press, 1983; *Readings for Year B,* 1984; *Readings for Year C,* 1985.

Kirk, James G. *When We Gather: A Book of Prayers for Worship,* Year A. Geneva Press, 1983; Year B, 1984; Year C, 1985.

The Service for the Lord's Day: The Worship of God. Supplemental Liturgical Resource 1. Westminster Press, 1984.

Music

Duck, Ruth C., and Michael G. Bausch, eds. *Everflowing Streams: Songs for Worship.* Pilgrim Press, 1981.

Emswiler, Sharon, and Tom Neufer, eds. *Sisters and Brothers Sing!* 2nd ed. Wesley Foundation Campus Ministry, 1977.

Huber, Jane Parker. *Fresh Words to Familiar Tunes.* United Presbyterian Women, 1982.

Lodge, Ann, comp. *Creation Sings.* Geneva Press, 1979.

Theological Studies and Sermon Preparation Aids

Fiorenza, Elisabeth Schüssler. *Bread Not Stone: The Challenge of Feminist Biblical Interpretation.* Beacon Press, 1985.

―――. *In Memory of Her: A Feminist Theological Reconstruction of Christian Origins.* Crossroad, 1983.

Mollenkott, Virginia Ramey. *The Divine Feminine: The Biblical Imagery of God as Female.* Crossroad, 1983.

Russell Letty M., ed. *Feminist Interpretation of the Bible.* Westminster Press, 1985.

―――, ed. *The Liberating Word: A Guide to Nonsexist Interpretation of the Bible.* Westminster Press, 1976.

Stagg, Evelyn, and Frank Stagg. *Woman in the World of Jesus.* Westminster Press, 1978.

Swidler, Leonard. *Biblical Affirmations of Woman.* Westminster Press, 1979.

Trible, Phyllis. *God and the Rhetoric of Sexuality.* Fortress Press,
    1978.
Wilson-Kastner, Patricia. *Faith, Feminism, and the Christ.* For-
    tress Press, 1983.

Additional Readings

Meadow, Mary Jo. "Wifely Submission: Psychological/Spiritual Growth Perspectives." *Journal of Religion & Health,* Summer 1980, pp. 103–120.

Miller, Alice. *For Your Own Good: Hidden Cruelty in Child-Rearing and the Roots of Violence.* Farrar, Straus & Giroux, 1983.

Monfalcone, Wesley R. *Coping with Abuse in the Family.* A Christian Care Book. Westminster Press, 1980.

Ochshorn, Judith. *The Female Experience and the Nature of the Divine.* Indiana University Press, 1981.

Pellauer, Mary. "Violence Against Women: The Theological Dimension." *Christianity and Crisis,* May 30, 1983, pp. 206–212.

Plaskow, Judith. *Sex, Sin, and Grace: Women's Experience and the Theologies of Reinhold Niebuhr and Paul Tillich.* University Press of America, 1980.

Russell, Letty M. *The Future of Partnership.* Westminster Press, 1979.

———. *Growth in Partnership.* Westminster Press, 1981.